Contents

Introduction

The Office of the Comptroller of the Currency's (OCC) *Comptroller's Handbook* booklet, "Retail Lending," is prepared for use by OCC examiners in connection with their examination and supervision of national banks and federal savings associations (collectively, banks). Each bank is different and may present specific issues. Accordingly, examiners should apply the information in this booklet consistent with each bank's individual circumstances. When it is necessary to distinguish between them, national banks and federal savings associations are referred to separately.

This booklet discusses risks associated with retail lending and provides a framework for evaluating risk management activities. This booklet supplements the core assessment in the "Large Bank Supervision," "Community Bank Supervision," and "Federal Branches and Agencies Supervision" booklets of the *Comptroller's Handbook*. Examiners should use this "Retail Lending" booklet when specific retail credit products, services, or risks warrant review beyond the core assessment.

This booklet's objective is to consider risk management practices fundamental to retail lending and common across product types. Additional product-specific considerations may apply. For example, certain lending and risk management practices relevant to particular products are described in other booklets of the *Comptroller's Handbook*, including "Residential Real Estate Lending," "Mortgage Banking," "Credit Card Lending," "Student Lending," and "Installment Lending." Specific consumer protection laws and regulations applicable to retail lending are discussed in the *Consumer Compliance* booklets of the *Comptroller's Handbook*.

In addition, the OCC has established minimum standards for designing and implementing a risk governance framework for certain large insured national banks, insured federal savings associations, and insured federal branches of foreign banks. Such institutions with average total consolidated assets of $50 billion or greater or those that are OCC-designated, which are referred to as covered banks, should adhere to 12 CFR 30, appendix D, "OCC Guidelines Establishing Heightened Standards for Certain Large Insured National Banks, Insured Federal Savings Associations, and Insured Federal Branches" (referred to in this booklet as heightened standards).[1] This booklet discusses these heightened standards in the context of retail lending, as well as broader concepts applicable to a wider range of banks.

Heightened Standards

Specific criteria for covered banks, subject to 12 CFR 30, appendix D, are noted in text boxes like this one throughout this booklet.

---

[1] Refer to OCC Bulletin 2014-45, "Heightened Standards for Large Banks; Integration of 12 CFR 30 and 12 CFR 170: Final Rules and Guidelines."

Overview

The OCC defines retail lending in OCC Bulletin 2000-20, "Uniform Retail Credit Classification and Account Management Policy: Policy Implementation," as closed- and open-end credit extended to individuals for household, family, and other personal expenditures. Retail lending products include consumer loans, credit cards, auto loans, student loans, and loans to individuals secured by their personal residences, including first mortgage, home equity, and home improvement loans.

Retail lending products may be either secured or unsecured, and the source of repayment is typically the borrower's employment-related income (or less frequently, the borrower's assets). Retail loan structures generally fall into one of two types: closed-end installment loans and open-end revolving lines of credit.

- **Closed-end installment loans** include loans made for a predetermined amount, with periodic payments of principal and interest over a specified term. Most often, the payments completely pay off the loan amount by the end of the term. In some cases, amortization schedules extend past the maturity date, leaving a lump sum (or balloon) payment due upon maturity. The finance charge may be a fixed or variable rate, and the borrower does not have the option of obtaining additional funds under the original loan agreement. Examples of closed-end installment loans include mortgage loans and auto loans.
- **Open-end revolving lines of credit** include amounts available to a borrower up to a preset credit limit for a specified amount of time. Balances may be drawn or paid down at any time at the borrower's option. Repayment terms typically require interest each month, and often some portion of principal as well. Some revolving lines of credit require full repayment of principal at maturity, while others convert automatically into a closed-end loan once the revolving period ends. Examples of open-end revolving lines of credit include credit cards and home equity lines of credit.

Banks offer retail lending products directly through a range of sources including branch offices and online banking platforms. Banks also use indirect origination sources,[2] such as automobile dealers, department stores, correspondent banks, and mortgage brokers. Each origination source has advantages and challenges, and most banks rely on more than one source to originate loans.

Numerous factors influence the demand for and availability of retail lending products. A borrower's income, age, life-cycle stage, lifestyle, attitudes about borrowing, and personal financial condition all affect the use of credit. Economic factors, such as inflation, interest rates, employment, and local economic conditions influence credit volumes and activity. Technology advances also permit retail lenders to better differentiate risk and to accept and price exposures more selectively. These advances promote the use of tailored products better

---

[2] Indirect lending generally refers to the use of a third party to originate loans using a bank's underwriting criteria. The third party receives a fee for providing an acceptable borrower. Indirect lending typically takes one of two forms: (1) dealers or brokers may originate loans to borrowers, and banks then purchase the loans or (2) dealers or brokers forward loan applications to banks that then originate the loans.

able to meet individual borrower risk profiles, allowing many banks to expand their markets and increase profitability.

This booklet describes prudent bank practices to manage retail credit risk appropriately. These include practices that examiners should consider when evaluating a bank's quantity of risk and quality of risk management.

Risks Associated With Retail Lending

From a supervisory perspective, risk is the potential that events will have an adverse effect on a bank's current or projected financial condition[3] and resilience.[4] The OCC has defined eight categories of risk for bank supervision purposes: credit, interest rate, liquidity, price, operational, compliance, strategic, and reputation. These categories are not mutually exclusive. Any product or service may expose the bank to multiple risks. Risks also may be interdependent and may be positively or negatively correlated. Examiners should be aware of this interdependence and assess the effect in a consistent and inclusive manner. Examiners also should be alert to concentrations that can significantly elevate risk. Concentrations can accumulate within and across products, business lines, geographic areas, countries, and legal entities. Refer to the "Bank Supervision Process" booklet of the *Comptroller's Handbook* for an expanded discussion of banking risks and their definitions.

While retail lending generally involves all risk categories, this booklet focuses on the significant credit, interest rate, operational, liquidity, compliance, strategic, and reputation risks most common to retail lending.

Credit Risk

Credit risk is the risk to earnings or capital arising from an obligor's failure to meet the terms of any contract with the bank or otherwise perform as agreed. Credit risk is the primary exposure for most retail lending products. Due to the size, volume, and nature of transactions, credit analysis is generally most rigorous at a retail loan's inception, with loan quality monitored over time through payment performance, periodically refreshed credit scores, and, when necessary, updated collateral valuations. Lenders seldom receive updated borrower income information to monitor ongoing capacity, so prudent loan structures and active credit administration are crucial. Retail portfolios typically consist of sizeable segments of relatively homogeneous loans, and credit risk analysis lends itself well to statistical techniques (e.g., scorecard models) to identify, manage, and control risk levels and exposures.

---

[3] Financial condition includes impacts from diminished capital and liquidity. Capital in this context includes potential impacts from losses, reduced earnings, and market value of equity.

[4] Resilience recognizes the bank's ability to withstand periods of stress.

Interest Rate Risk

Interest rate risk is the risk to earnings or capital arising from movements in interest rates. Interest rate risk arises from differences in the timing of rate changes and the timing of cash flows, from changing rate relationships among yield curves, from changing rate relationships across maturities, and from interest-related embedded options in bank products. The level of interest rate risk depends on the composition of the bank's loan portfolio and the degree to which loan terms (e.g., maturity, rate structure, and embedded options) expose the bank or its borrowers to changes in interest rates. Many borrowers prefer fixed interest rates on larger, long-term retail loans, such as first mortgages and automobile loans. Long-term fixed-rate loans require active asset-liability management by bank management, because core deposits used to fund retail portfolios typically have a variable interest rate. Borrowers may also assume interest rate risk on such products as home equity lines of credit (HELOC). In this context, interest rate risk is the risk of higher monthly payments on variable rate loans due to rising interest rates, a factor that may also increase credit risk for affected loans. Banks should identify borrowers with heightened exposure to interest rate changes and consider the impact on these borrowers' ability to repay if interest rates were to increase. The "Interest Rate Risk" booklet of the *Comptroller's Handbook* provides additional guidance on interest rate risk management.

Operational Risk

Operational risk is the risk to earnings or capital arising from inadequate or failed internal processes or systems, inappropriate accounting, human errors or misconduct, or adverse external events. Operational risk in retail lending is often elevated with higher volumes of loans, larger numbers of transactions processed, and more extensive use of automation and technology. Highly automated environments such as retail lending pose heightened operational risk exposure since issues in this area tend to affect numerous transactions and may compound the exposure of even minor errors. To control exposure and manage risks, outsourcing operational functions (e.g., loan origination, account management, collections, payment processing, data input, and legal assistance) to third parties should include due diligence before establishing third-party relationships.

Liquidity Risk

Liquidity risk is the risk to current or projected financial condition and resilience arising from an inability to meet obligations when they come due. Liquidity risk includes the inability to access funding sources or manage fluctuations in funding levels. Liquidity risk in retail credit depends largely on the types of products offered and the manner in which they are funded. Retail portfolios are typically funded through the bank's deposit base, securitizing loans, or a combination of the two. Liquidity risk may arise from a bank's failure to recognize or address changes in market conditions that affect its ability to liquidate assets quickly and with minimal loss in value. Liquidity risk is also present in a bank's obligation to fund undrawn portions of open-ended credit, such as credit cards or HELOCs.

Compliance Risk

Compliance risk is the risk to earnings or capital arising from violations of laws or regulations, or from nonconformance with prescribed practices, internal policies and procedures, or ethical standards. Because of the number of consumer protection laws and regulations, banks engaged in retail lending are highly vulnerable to compliance risk. Some federal consumer protection laws relevant to retail lending include the Equal Credit Opportunity Act, Fair Housing Act, Fair Credit Reporting Act, Fair Debt Collection Practices Act of 1977, Truth in Lending Act, Real Estate Settlement Procedures Act, Military Lending Act, Servicemembers Civil Relief Act of 2003, and laws prohibiting unfair, deceptive, or abusive acts or practices.[5] Banks also have obligations arising from the Bank Secrecy Act of 1970 (BSA) and the sanctions laws administered by the U.S. Department of the Treasury's Office of Financial Assets Control.

Strategic Risk

Strategic risk is the risk to earnings, capital, or enterprise value arising from adverse business decisions, poor implementation of business decisions, or lack of responsiveness to changes in the banking industry and operating environment. A bank's board and management decisions to enter, exit, or otherwise change the bank's participation in retail markets and products should be based on sound, complete information, realistic assessments of the risks involved, management's expertise, and the bank's practical operating capacity. Incomplete or inadequate consideration of the industry's market conditions, economic dynamics, and consumer behaviors expose the bank to unnecessary or unanticipated strategic risk, which often translates into financial losses.

Reputation Risk

Reputation risk is the risk to earnings, capital, or enterprise value arising from negative public opinion. This risk may impair the bank's competitiveness by affecting its ability to establish new relationships or services or continue servicing existing relationships. Inadequate policies and procedures, operational breakdowns, or general weaknesses in any aspect of the bank's retail lending activities can harm its reputation. Inappropriate delegation of activities to third parties and wrongful acts by third parties acting on the bank's behalf may also increase a bank's reputation risk exposure. Effective systems and controls to identify, measure, monitor, and control potential issues, such as appropriate oversight of sales, servicing, and collection practices, are critical to managing reputation risk.

---

[5] For more information about consumer protection laws and regulations, refer to the *Consumer Compliance* booklets of the *Comptroller's Handbook*, including "Compliance Management System," "Fair Credit Reporting," "Fair Lending," "Other Consumer Protection Laws and Regulations," "Servicemembers Civil Relief Act of 2003," and "Truth in Lending Act."

Risk Management

Each bank's board and management should identify, measure, monitor, and control risk by implementing an effective risk management system appropriate for the size and complexity of its operations. When examiners assess the effectiveness of the bank's risk management practices, they consider the bank's policies, processes, personnel, and control systems. Refer to the "Bank Supervision Process" booklet of the *Comptroller's Handbook* for an expanded discussion of risk management.

Elements of a Sound Risk Management Framework

The OCC expects risk management for retail lending activities to correspond to the bank's size, complexity, and risk profile. Examiners should assess risk management practices in the context of inherent product and portfolio risk. While risk management objectives are similar for most banks, specific practices may differ depending on the products offered, the volume and types of transactions, and the markets targeted. Community banks with a low quantity of risk may operate with less sophisticated risk management frameworks.[6] Large banks, or those with higher-risk or complex products, should have more sophisticated frameworks. Primary examination objectives are to understand how each bank identifies and manages the risk inherent in the bank's portfolio, and whether risk management practices are effective in the context of the risks assumed.

The board has a critical role in overseeing the retail credit approval and risk management functions of the bank. Directors should regularly question the propriety of strategic initiatives, staffing and management decisions, and the balance between risk taking and profitability. Most importantly, they should recognize the need to establish a risk management framework that effectively assesses risks, monitors exposures, and adopts the necessary policies and procedures for operating the retail business in a sound and prudent manner. Informed directors also understand that the framework should be consistent with the bank's size, complexity, and risk profile, and that most sound frameworks have certain common elements. One primary examination objective is to determine whether these elements are present, and whether the operating processes are reliable under day-to-day and stressful conditions. While practices vary, there are basic characteristics that generally reflect a well-managed retail credit portfolio. These include

- structured oversight by the board and senior management.
- clear and consistent policies and operating procedures.
- a well-established risk appetite.
- structured risk assessments.
- well-defined processes for policy exceptions.

---

[6] This booklet applies to all banks with retail lending activities. The OCC expects community banks to have risk management practices commensurate with the level of risk and complexity of the banks' retail lending activities. The OCC recognizes that the risk management systems of community banks may not be as sophisticated as those of complex banks. In most cases, the fundamental aspects discussed apply. Community banks' boards and management should identify retail lending activities that involve critical activities and ensure the banks have risk management practices to assess, monitor, and manage the risks.

- effective monitoring reports.
- well-designed strategies, business plans, and product testing.

Heightened Standards

A covered bank should establish and adhere to a formal, written risk governance framework that is designed by independent risk management and approved by the board of directors or the board's risk committee. The risk governance framework should include delegations of authority from the board to management committees and executive officers as well as the risk limits established for material activities. Independent risk management should review and update the framework at least annually, and as often as needed to address improvements in industry risk management practices and changes in the covered bank's risk profile caused by emerging risks, its strategic plans, or other internal and external factors.[7]

Structured Oversight by the Board and Senior Management

One of the board and senior management's most important oversight responsibilities is to establish an effective risk management framework consistent with the bank's risk profile. Characteristics of sound oversight include the following.

- **Properly approved policies and procedures:** The board (or a board-designated committee) should approve all credit policies at least annually, or whenever a significant change occurs. Policies should be clearly written and consistent with the established risk appetite and desired risk profile. The board also should expect regular updates on the volume, performance, and potential impact of credit policy exceptions.
- **Established risk and product committees:** Product and risk oversight committees serve as active forums to discuss risks and emerging issues, provide a broad spectrum of input, and evaluate or approve decisions. Community banks that have small, non-complex loan portfolios may have fewer committees with broader responsibilities, while larger banks may have product-specific committees with narrower scopes. Committee charters should define required membership, frequency of meetings and reports, documentation of minutes, and committee responsibilities and accountabilities. Committee responsibilities often encompass both risk and business management objectives, and membership should include individuals with the knowledge and experience for the tasks.
- **Clear lines of authority, responsibility, and accountability:** Roles and responsibilities across the retail lending business should be well-defined and well-communicated. Business managers should identify and assess material risks, operate within the parameters of an established risk appetite, and adhere to established policies and operating procedures. An independent credit and risk management review process should assess credit risk independent of the business units,[8] monitor compliance with concentration and risk limits, and raise issues directly to senior management, oversight

---

[7] For more information, refer to 12 CFR 30, appendix D, II.A, "Risk Governance Framework."

[8] For most banks, an independent risk management function or process is an important and necessary control. Some community banks with standard products and low-risk concentration levels may operate prudently without an independent risk management function. These banks, however, should maintain appropriate internal controls and internal audit coverage of retail lending activities.

committees, and the board. Internal audit and other independent control functions should evaluate the adequacy of established policies and procedures and identify noncompliance with the risk governance framework.

- **Established risk appetite:**[9] A risk appetite statement establishes a common understanding within the bank on how management should approach and accept risks when executing the bank's strategy and business plan. Risk appetite statements generally include acceptable risks the bank intends to take because the risk is sufficiently compensated and unacceptable risks that should be avoided or heavily mitigated. Used properly, the risk appetite statement is an important and powerful way to communicate risk-reward tradeoffs, establish risk capacity, and define risk tolerances that should not be exceeded without proper escalation and approval.

Heightened Standards

A covered bank's board of directors should actively oversee the covered bank's risk-taking activities and hold management accountable for adhering to the risk governance framework. In providing active oversight, the directors may rely on risk assessments and reports prepared by independent risk management and internal audit to support the bank's ability to question, challenge, and when necessary, oppose recommendations and decisions made by management that could cause the covered bank's risk profile to exceed its risk appetite or jeopardize the safety and soundness of the covered bank.[10]

Clear and Consistent Policies and Operating Procedures

Lending policies and operating procedures help employees make consistent decisions, providing a sound foundation for sustainably profitable operations. Examiners should expect the board to set broad policy goals, and senior management to develop specific policies and operating procedures that promote effective day-to-day execution. Policies can vary among banks but should always be commensurate with the bank's size, risk profile, portfolio objectives, core competencies, products offered, and target markets. Once policies and operating procedures have been developed, the board and senior management should hold bank personnel accountable for compliance, while also providing a practical avenue for handling exceptions.

Policies should cover all aspects of credit risk management, including credit approvals, credit administration, oversight, and internal controls, and should be consistent with applicable laws, regulations, and guidelines. Operating procedures should complement credit policies and describe how each policy is put into practice. Procedures should provide details on job responsibilities, approval authorities, necessary steps for approvals, and approval

---

[9] Risk appetite refers to the aggregate level and types of risk the board and senior management are willing to assume to achieve the bank's strategic objectives and business plan, consistent with applicable capital, liquidity, and other regulatory requirements. Smaller community banks may not have a formal risk appetite statement; however, board-approved policies and procedures should include sufficient discussion of the board's appetite for retail credit risk.

[10] For more information, refer to 12 CFR 30, appendix D, III.B, "Provide Active Oversight of Management."

documentation requirements.[11] Process maps, which link directly to operating procedures, provide a third level of detail and documentation on how and when specific actions occur. The discipline of committing policies, procedures, and process maps to writing promotes a deeper understanding of each activity, and prompts a practical evaluation of how each step contributes to or detracts from business and risk management objectives.[12] Examiners should view evidence of well-written and cohesive policies, procedures, and process maps as part of an effective risk management process, and the absence of such evidence as a potential deficiency.

Policy criteria should be consistent with and support established risk appetites and portfolio objectives. For example, banks with low risk appetites may have product underwriting standards that require higher down payments, use lower debt-to-income ratios, or are less tolerant of derogatory information on credit reports. Banks with higher risk appetites might accept lower down payments, use higher debt-to-income ratios, or consider some negative credit bureau information. Either may be acceptable, depending on the bank's resources, quality of risk management, and internal controls. Policies should be directly reconcilable with the bank's risk appetite and business operating plans.

Heightened Standards

Each frontline unit should establish and adhere to a set of written policies that ensure risks associated with the frontline unit's activities are effectively identified, measured, monitored, and controlled, consistent with the covered bank's risk appetite statement, concentration risk limits, and all policies established within the risk governance framework.[13]

Well-Developed Risk Appetite

The OCC defines risk appetite as the aggregate level and types of risk the board and senior management are willing to assume to achieve the bank's strategic objectives and business plan, consistent with applicable capital, liquidity, and other regulatory requirements.[14] Well-conceived risk appetite statements establish a common understanding within the bank on how management should approach and accept risks when executing the bank's strategy and

---

[11] These items may be incorporated into policies rather than operating procedures at some community banks.

[12] The size and complexity of many community banks may not necessitate the use of process maps for some or any processes.

[13] For more information, refer to 12 CFR 30, appendix D, II.C.1, "Roles and Responsibilities of Front Line Units."

[14] For more information on establishing a risk appetite, refer to the "Corporate and Risk Governance" booklet of the *Comptroller's Handbook,* OCC Bulletin 2014-45, "Heightened Standards for Large Banks; Integration of 12 CFR 30 and 12 CFR 170: Final Rules and Guidelines," and 12 CFR 30, appendix D, "OCC Guidelines Establishing Heightened Standards for Certain Large Insured National Banks, Insured Federal Savings Associations, and Insured Federal Branches." While the OCC's Heightened Standards in 12 CFR 30, appendix D, apply only to banks of a certain size, they may provide additional information or examples of prudent practices for institutions not covered by appendix D.

business plan. Specific assertions generally include acceptable risks the board intends the bank to take, and unacceptable risks that should be avoided or heavily mitigated. Most importantly, the bank's risk appetite should provide high-level support for the bank's business strategies, as well as provide context for management decisions as issues and business opportunities arise. Used properly, an established risk appetite is an important and powerful way to communicate risk-reward tradeoffs, establish risk capacity, and define risk tolerances.

There are many ways to approach establishing a risk appetite, and the structure and formality should be consistent with the bank's size, complexity, and risk profile.[15] The board of a bank with smaller, non-complex, or lower-risk retail portfolios may choose to establish a risk appetite at the bank level, and then management can reconcile retail credit business plans to determine consistency with the overall risk appetite. Boards and management at banks with large, complex, or high-risk retail credit portfolios should consider establishing written risk appetite statements at the retail lending level and should manage product- and service-level activities from that base (e.g., risk appetite limits cascade to individual portfolios with tiered oversight, monitoring, and reporting). The terminology may differ from bank to bank, but the basic characteristics should be discernable, complementary, and include practical expressions of the bank's retail risk strategy, tolerances, preferences, and limits. These characteristics may include the following:

Retail risk strategies that definitively state the board and senior management's views on risk, including how the bank will assume retail exposure. Risk strategies generally set broad parameters, expressing how the bank intends to limit or mitigate risks to reduce the likelihood of insolvency or significant losses.

Retail risk tolerances that are a quantitative extension of the risk strategy. Risk tolerances quantify the amount of aggregate risk the bank is willing to accept, and the critical areas where it chooses not to accept exposure. For example, a retail lending business might set risk tolerances for capital maintenance, measured on a nominal or risk-adjusted basis; financial performance, measured by risk-adjusted returns; liquidity, including minimum buffers and access to markets; and franchise value, measured by customer satisfaction surveys, customer complaint levels, or other measures of reputation risk. Risk tolerances within the risk appetite statement are generally set for only a few key factors that relate directly to business or mission failure. Most importantly, risk tolerances should be measureable, so that actual levels of risk can be monitored to provide certainty that standards are not breached.

Retail risk preferences that reflect where the business has (or perceives itself to have) competitive advantages and may pursue risk. Risk preferences for a retail lender often include specific products, target markets, or delivery channels.

Retail risk attractiveness, which focuses on tactical rankings of the risk strategy and risk preference options. Risk attractiveness ranks the relative appeal of opportunities according to

---

[15] Small community banks may not have a formal risk appetite statement; however, board-approved policies and procedures should include sufficient discussion of the board's appetite for retail credit risk.

current conditions, and translates risk preferences into current business plans.[16] Risk attractiveness rankings vary among banks, even of the same size and geographic areas. This may be due, for example, to available resources, staff expertise, or management and the board's view on market and economic conditions.

Retail risk limits that are capacity controls to manage risk levels. Risk limits are set for specific risk sources, business units, or products, and help implement the higher-level risk tolerances. Some banks use their stress testing results to establish aggregate and product risk capacity, translating results into operational capacity limits. Risk limits complement the risk tolerances and are generally more granular, practical controls at the portfolio and sub-portfolio levels, using metrics that can be managed at the business-line level.

Practical risk appetite statements generally result from analysis and consideration of each of these risk characteristics. Each helps management understand and articulate parameters for managing the business and assuming risk. Examiners may see different terms and labels for these characteristics, but should expect to see the essentials of each as part of the risk assessment exercise that establishes the bank's risk appetite statement.

Heightened Standards

A covered bank should have a comprehensive written statement that articulates the covered bank's risk appetite and serves as the basis for the risk governance framework. The risk appetite statement should include both qualitative components and quantitative limits. The qualitative components should describe a safe and sound risk culture and how the covered bank will assess and accept risks, including those that are difficult to quantify. Quantitative limits should incorporate sound stress testing processes, as appropriate, and address the covered bank's earnings, capital, and liquidity. The covered bank should set limits at levels that take into account appropriate capital and liquidity buffers and prompt management and the board of directors to reduce risk before the covered bank's risk profile jeopardizes the adequacy of its earnings, liquidity, and capital.[17]

Structured Risk Assessment

Developing an effective retail risk appetite requires a practical, realistic assessment of risks facing the business. One common method is through risk assessment exercises. These exercises are designed to consider the potential impact of events that could significantly affect the bank. Approaches vary, but most assessments consider four key threat aspects: the risk event, likelihood of occurrence, practical impact, and significance. Table 1 provides an example of risks a retail lender might consider during a credit risk assessment exercise.

---

[16] For example, a home equity lender might rate high-balance HELOCs highly in risk attractiveness because they are a customer relationship and cross-selling vehicle, but not closed-end home equity loans because management may believe that customers view such loans solely as down-payment alternatives and the loans have no real relationship benefits for the lender.

[17] For more information, refer to 12 CFR 30, appendix D, II.E, "Risk Appetite Statement."

Table 1: Credit Risk Assessment Exercise Example

Risk event	Likelihood	Impact	Significance
Significant new technology advancement or application that changes how retail lending products are marketed, priced, and delivered to consumers.	Low, moderate	20 percent revenue reduction for the next year due to new competitors and the need to update delivery channels.	Material shortfall in revenues and business profitability. May require reexamining the business model and competitive approach.
Disruption in the mortgage insurance industry that limits availability or significantly increases costs.	Low	25 percent reduction in origination volumes. 10 percent increase in capital requirements from keeping greater origination volumes on balance sheet.	Could change fundamental operation of residential mortgage markets. Higher cost of insurance. Significant secondary market disruption until alternative sources emerge. Potential opportunity to selectively expand market share in profitable target markets if the bank is willing to use balance-sheet capacity.
Changes in the reliability or timeliness of credit information available from credit bureaus or other third-party sources.	Low, moderate	Significant potential impact on credit scores and reliability of credit bureau information for estimating risk.	Potential serious setback for consumer lending in the United States. May prompt search to find alternative methods or sources of reliable performance information.
Changes in the bankruptcy laws that limit or expand certain forms of bankruptcy use by consumers.	Low	Greater shift to co-borrower reliance, lower total debt advances, underwriting more closely tied to shorter-term capacity.	Potential for significant initial disruption unless existing loans are grandfathered. Controllable if implemented prospectively, but volumes and average loan amounts are likely to decline.
Rapid increase in short-term interest rates that influence consumer-credit pricing indexes.	Moderate, high	10 percent increase in credit card revenues, 2 percent increase in cost of funds, 5 percent increase in 30+ delinquencies.	As long as interest rate increases are moderate, for example, no more than 100 basis points, the increase in revenues should offset the higher delinquency rates. Creates a need to monitor both measures closely.
A local military base, the largest employer in the community, may be relocated or substantially reduced within the next three years.	Moderate, high	20 percent increase in local unemployment, 25 percent decline in auto and installment loan volumes, 10 percent decline in checking and savings account volumes.	Significant impact on borrowers employed by the base. Decline in new loan business and checking and savings accounts. Will affect small businesses that serve customers living and working on the base. Creates a need to monitor closely and join local government efforts to lobby against closure.

The risk event column of table 1 considers risks significant enough to potentially threaten or change the bank's business strategy. The likelihood column considers the probability of occurrence, and can be qualitative (high, moderate, or low) or quantitative (5 percent chance of occurring). The impact column focuses primarily on the event's direct effect on the business, and the significance column focuses on how results are likely to affect business strategies or major objectives. Other factors can be part of the risk assessment exercise, such as a residual risk rating that considers risk levels after controls or other mitigating factors are taken into account. Examiners should consider whether each bank's exercise is a practical, thoughtful, and systematic approach to identifying and considering risk. Factors to consider include whether a reasonably wide range of primary threats is considered, all important risk events have been identified, risks are monitored on a continual basis, potential exposures have been quantified after consideration of likelihood and impact, and responses are reasonable and appropriate.

The results of the risk assessment process should help management design appropriate business responses to available opportunities. Responses generally fall within one of four categories:

- **Avoidance:** When risks cannot be adequately controlled or measured. Avoidance might include exiting a business line or geographic segment after appropriate evaluation of the risks, or deciding not to engage in a new product or service.
- **Mitigation:** When risk levels can be adequately managed internally, or shared or controlled by third parties. Sharing might include insurance, partnerships, hedging, outsourcing, or other risk transfer methods.
- **Reduction:** When risk levels can be managed to within acceptable tolerances, generally through risk, concentration, or operational limits. Reduction often includes diversification limits, business rules, and portfolio rebalancing to reduce vulnerability to certain types of exposures.
- **Acceptance:** When risk levels can be consciously tolerated or self-insured because the probability and severity are within reasonable limits. Banks sometimes accept risks because there are natural internal offsets, such as variable rate deposits funding variable rate loans.

Examiners should expect risk assessment exercises to be a regular part of the risk appetite and business strategy development. The structure and formality depend on the bank's size, complexity, and risk profile. Banks with large, complex retail portfolios should have enhanced[18] risk appetite and risk assessment processes and documentation, and these estimates should work in concert with the bank's stress testing processes. Even for small banks, examiners should see indications of the risk assessment process in discussions with management, committee meeting minutes, management reports, or other discussion or risk management documentation.

Well-Defined Policy Exception Protocols

The bank's underwriting policies, operating policies, and credit criteria should closely reflect its stated risk appetite and desired risk profile. Consequently, policy exceptions have the potential to change the actual risk profile of the portfolio and present credit, strategic, and compliance risk. Once policies are in place, the board should generally expect management to operate within those standards.

Well-run banks generally handle exceptions in a structured and disciplined manner to promote sound operations as well as compliance with fair lending and other laws and regulations. Responsibility and authority for identifying, approving, and monitoring policy exceptions should be in writing, with regular reporting to capture exceptions at the

---

[18] "Enhanced" processes and documentation generally refer to the depth of analysis, level of sophistication, and formality and structure of activities. As retail portfolios become larger or more complex, examiners should expect to see better documentation and structure for activities to support effective risk management.

transaction, product segment, product, and portfolio levels. Most banks require enhanced analysis when exception volumes reach established thresholds, and results of the analysis should be an important factor in policy updates or revisions.

Policy exception volumes and analysis should be a normal part of board and senior management reporting. Policy compliance is an essential risk management tool, and examiners should view adherence to the exceptions process as an important internal control. Some exceptions will occur, because it is nearly impossible to construct underwriting or operating policies covering every lending situation. Still, exception types and volumes should be controlled, with appropriate reporting to identify and track exceptions and appropriate analysis to determine causes, impact, and any need for corrective action.

Policy exceptions for retail lending typically fall into three categories:

- **Credit policy:** Loan-to-value (LTV), debt-to-income, pricing, verification, etc.
- **Credit scoring:** High- and low-side overrides.[19]
- **Documentation:** Loan application, transaction information, and collateral perfection or valuation.

Exception limits for each, and in aggregate, are typically established by either dollar amounts or transaction volumes per month.[20] Trends can vary between dollar and transaction volumes, and banks with larger or more complex portfolios should typically track and evaluate both. Exception monitoring reports should include sufficient detail for meaningful analysis of exceptions overall and by type. The objective is to determine whether exceptions are significantly changing the risk profile of the portfolio, positively or negatively. To make this determination, assessments should consider the volume and trends of exceptions and the ongoing performance of loans approved with exceptions (including loans with multiple exceptions[21]). If long-term performance of an exception segment is weaker than expected or inconsistent with the bank's risk appetite, management should require stricter adherence to policy. If performance is better, management may consider policy revisions.

---

[19] A credit score override occurs when a lender approves a loan that does not meet the lender's minimum credit score (i.e., a low-side override), or declines a loan that was above the lender's minimum credit score (i.e., a high-side override). High-side overrides typically occur because a borrower fails some other aspect of the underwriting criteria, such as insufficient income or a recent bankruptcy. Non-complex community banks generally only track low-side overrides.

[20] Some smaller community banks may track exceptions less frequently than monthly because the volumes are small and monthly tracking would not typically produce a meaningful metric. These banks may use other frequencies and methods, such as tracking exceptions as a percentage of loans outstanding, that may be more meaningful to the size of their retail operations.

[21] In general, the presence of multiple policy exceptions in a single transaction increases risk and raises the likelihood that the transaction will be inconsistent with the bank's desired risk profile. Retail lenders should periodically evaluate risk levels for loans with multiple policy exceptions and consider limits on the number or type of exceptions permitted per transaction where warranted.

Effective Monitoring Reports

Management at most banks monitors credit performance and portfolio quality through standard reports measuring portfolio composition, borrower and portfolio performance, and policy compliance. Reports should be timely, accurate, and complete, and should provide information needed for sound management and credible challenges. A set of well-designed standard reports should monitor activity continually, even if the data seem stable. Consistent reporting allows managers to gain a comfort level with the information, ask insightful questions, and request additional facts or analysis when issues warrant.

Effective reporting generally includes four common characteristics that improve utility.

- **Performance trends:** Providing data in a consistent form over time helps provide perspective and a deeper understanding of portfolio composition and migration. Most banks report performance trends for at least the past 13 months, but many retail managers find trends over a rolling eight-quarter time frame most useful for considering patterns and seasonality.
- **Actual results compared with projections:** Context is important. Effective reports compare actual results with management expectations and quantitative benchmarks, with variances identified and explained.
- **Precise and informative narrative:** Useful data charts generally include narrative, especially in reports for senior management and the board. Rather than require readers to make assumptions, reports walk the user through the issue or topic in a logical, intuitive manner. The more distanced the user is from day-to-day management of an issue, the more simple, clear, and direct the narrative should be.
- **Segmented performance:** Segmentation refers to breaking down aggregate data into smaller subpopulations for analysis and monitoring. Aggregated data should be segmented whenever performance could reasonably be expected to differ, allowing patterns that might otherwise be diluted by aggregated data to become more readily apparent. For example, new loans could be tracked by acquisition source, vintage, geography, or other common characteristics, so users can identify segments with weak performance or issues needing attention.

When possible, a single data source is best for reporting consistency. When this is not possible, data sources should be periodically reconciled and audited to determine reliability. Risk managers should ensure that reporting allows senior management and the board to monitor information necessary to control risks within the bank. For banks with large or complex retail portfolios, key risk reporting (such as compliance with risk appetite measures) is often developed and reported by an independent risk management function.

> **Heightened Standards**
>
> The risk governance framework should include a set of policies, supported by appropriate procedures and processes, designed to provide risk data aggregation and reporting capabilities appropriate for the size, complexity, and risk profile of the covered bank, and to support supervisory reporting requirements. Collectively, these policies, procedures, and processes should provide for the following:
>
> - Design, implementation, and maintenance of a data architecture and information technology infrastructure that supports the covered bank's risk aggregation and reporting needs during both normal times and times of stress.
> - Capturing and aggregating of risk data and reporting of material risks, concentrations, and emerging risks in a timely manner to the board of directors and the OCC.
> - Distribution of risk reports to all relevant parties at a frequency that meets the needs for decision-making purposes.[22]

Well-Designed Strategies and Business Plans

Strategic plans define the bank's desired role in the retail markets. A retail strategy should state the bank's intent by product type, economic sector, geographic location, currency, maturity, and anticipated profitability. Decisions to offer a new product, significantly change terms on an existing product, or expand into a new market area are strategic decisions that should be supported by sound and documented analysis and due diligence. This analysis extends to the risk assessment exercise and typically addresses

- competitive environment.
- capabilities and expertise.
- operational capacity.
- staffing and training needs.
- control systems in place and those needed.
- compliance requirements.
- reporting and operational systems.
- financial projections.

Once senior management and the board adopt strategic objectives, business line managers prepare complementary business plans for each major product. Business plan development should involve knowledgeable staff from key functional areas, including risk management, credit policy, marketing, systems, operations, training, finance or accounting, legal, compliance, internal audit, quality assurance, and, if appropriate, third-party relationship management. Individuals representing each area should have strong knowledge of their area's resources and capabilities so they can provide informed input into business plans and proposals. The use of cross-functional teams helps form realistic and actionable business plans, promotes buy-in from important parties, and minimizes unanticipated problems during implementation.

---

[22] For more information, refer to 12 CFR 30, appendix D, II.J, "Risk Data Aggregation and Reporting."

Common topics in retail business plans address

- product design, marketing, and customer mix and profile.
- volume and profitability projections.
- product testing parameters.
- concentration and risk limits.
- capital and allowance requirements.
- reporting content and distribution.
- key performance monitoring measures.

Before implementation, management should reconcile business plans with existing lending and operating policies for comprehensive coverage and consistency. Bank staff should be thoroughly briefed and trained on any changes, with reporting systems and internal controls fully tested and operational. Examiners should pay particular attention to how banks implement new business strategies, including the rollout of new products or initiatives.[23] This is especially important when changes could significantly affect the bank's size, operating approach, or risk profile. Examiners should consider whether effective change management processes exist, including realistic assessments of costs and resource requirements (including information technology requirements); adequate testing periods; timely and accurate performance monitoring; and effective policies, operating procedures, and internal controls.

Even after business plans are developed, the board, or a designated board committee, should make certain that senior management is fully capable of managing credit activities within the approved risk strategy, policies, and tolerances. Compensation policies should not contradict the credit risk strategy. Red flags generally include focusing on loan production at the expense of loan quality, generating nominal profits while deviating from credit policies, or exceeding established limits.[24] In addition, for residential real estate-secured lending, loan officer compensation policies must comply with the requirements of Regulation Z, which implements the Truth in Lending Act.[25] All such practices affect the bank's credit processes. The board should monitor these practices closely and act on any deviations.

---

[23] For more information, refer to OCC Bulletin 2004-20, "Risk Management of New, Expanded, or Modified Bank Products and Services: Risk Management Process" (May 10, 2004) (national banks). For federal savings associations, refer to the *Office of Thrift Supervision (OTS) Examination Handbook*, section 760, "New Activities and Services" (September 2009).

[24] The OCC expects national banking organizations to regularly review their incentive compensation arrangements for all executive and non-executive employees who, either individually or as part of a group, have the ability to expose the organizations to material amounts of risk. The organizations also are expected to regularly review the risk management, control, and corporate governance processes related to these arrangements. Refer to OCC Bulletin 2010-24, "Incentive Compensation: Interagency Guidance on Sound Incentive Compensation Policies."

[25] Refer to 15 USC 1639b(c) (Truth in Lending Act) and 12 CFR 1026.36(d) (Regulation Z).

Heightened Standards

The chief executive officer (CEO) should be responsible for the development of a written strategic plan with input from frontline units, independent risk management, and internal audit. The board of directors should evaluate and approve the strategic plan and monitor management's efforts to implement the strategic plan at least annually.

The strategic plan should cover, at a minimum, a three-year period and

- contain a comprehensive assessment of risks that currently have an impact on the covered bank or that could have an impact on the covered bank during the period covered by the strategic plan.
- articulate an overall mission statement and strategic objectives for the covered bank, and include an explanation of how the covered bank will achieve those objectives.
- explain how the covered bank will update, as necessary, the risk governance framework to account for changes in the covered bank's risk profile projected under the strategic plan.
- be reviewed, updated, and approved, as necessary, due to changes in the covered bank's risk profile or operating environment that were not contemplated when the strategic plan was developed.[26]

Considering Quantity of Risk

The OCC expects risk management for retail credit activities to correspond to the bank's size, complexity, and risk profile. Examiners should assess risk management practices in the context of product and portfolio risk. For examination purposes, the OCC refers to the bank's inherent risk profile as the quantity of risk.

There are many ways to assess the bank's risk profile, and examiners should have active discussions with management and the board about how and where the bank assumes risk. For retail credit, discussions often focus on four key areas: risk in products and loan structures, risk in target markets, risk in credit underwriting due diligence, and risk layering—or combinations of these key areas. These discussions are often subjective, requiring judgment and experience to support proper risk assessment designations. Some risk always exists when extending credit, and these discussions are more about determining the appropriateness of risk management practices given the bank's existing and intended risk profile than attempting to set an absolute risk level.[27]

Risk in Loan Structures

Loan structures are the simplest starting point for evaluating retail credit risk. Generally, one of the lowest-risk loan structures is a fixed-rate installment loan that fully amortizes the loan amount over a short term. Each characteristic contributes to a lower-risk loan structure. The fixed interest rate eliminates rate exposure for the borrower and adds stability to the payment stream. Full amortization allows the borrower to demonstrate a willingness and capacity to repay each month, allowing delinquency to be a reliable indicator of loan quality. A short loan term (or reasonable term for the loan's purpose) increases the likelihood of full repayment under the economic and financial circumstances considered in the initial credit

---

[26] For more information, refer to 12 CFR 30, appendix D, II.D, "Strategic Plan."

[27] Appendix B of this booklet provides a supplemental matrix for assessing quantity of risk.

decision. All things being equal, portfolios dominated by this loan structure tend to have the lowest quantity of risk, and the quantity of risk assessment should scale from there.

Some product structure characteristics may contribute to risk if used improperly. For example, when used properly, loan pricing provides a portfolio-level cash flow buffer that helps mitigate inherent product risk. Credit cards are a good example. They are generally priced well even during recessions, and normal pricing of the product allows card portfolios to be profitable even though the underlying loans usually have the highest individual loss rates of any consumer product. Contrast this product with HELOCs, which are often lower-priced because of the existence of collateral and its perceived place in the borrower's payment hierarchy. Even high-LTV HELOCs typically receive low interest rates. When housing markets decline, many home equity lenders find themselves with partially secured exposures priced as if fully secured, a condition that detracts from portfolio stability over time.

Payment deferral features (e.g., loans with interest-only payments, delayed initial payments, balloon payments, or negative amortizations) also have higher risk and should include mitigating factors. The most significant issue is the lack of direct evidence from the borrower each month about orderly repayment willingness and capacity. Even loans that amortize, but have extended maturities, pose increased risk. The longer loan balances remain outstanding, the more susceptible they are to income declines, uncontrolled debt accumulation, collateral beyond or approaching its useful life, and other borrower life events such as illness, bankruptcy, or job loss. This issue is increasingly common when loan marketing focuses on monthly payment amounts, usually at the expense of other loan terms, such as maturities. For example, heightened risk is often evident when existing auto loan balances must be rolled into new auto loans because borrowers sought to buy a new car before the previous one was completely paid off. Examiners should expect bank management to identify, consider, and mitigate these types of risks whenever they become apparent.

Risk in Target Markets

Many banks focus mostly on higher-credit-quality, or prime, borrowers for their retail portfolios. Prime borrowers demonstrate a reliable payment history and the discipline to manage credit responsibly. Other banks focus on lower-credit-quality portfolios, commonly referred to as subprime, non-prime, or near prime. Most often, credit scores distinguish the segments, although other defining characteristics exist. In general, lower-credit-quality borrowers have higher inherent risk based on their past patterns of performance. Managed prudently, even a lower-credit-quality portfolio can be profitable, but stronger risk management practices are appropriate to mitigate the higher inherent credit risk.

Enhanced risk management practices are also appropriate when target markets change and a portfolio's mix evolves. This need for enhanced risk management is most notable when banks expand from prime to non-prime markets, as credit administration and collection practices can be markedly different. Prime lenders cannot simply migrate their business practices to non-prime segments and expect the same level of performance. This vulnerability is most notable when banks "drift" out of prime markets (i.e., incrementally expand their credit criteria) because of competition or declining profitability. Changing target markets can be a legitimate portfolio strategy but also can result in a higher quantity of risk. Examiners should watch for this migration and consider whether risk management practices are adjusting to account for portfolio changes.

Risk in Credit Underwriting Due Diligence

The diligence surrounding credit decisions is an important aspect of credit risk management. A sound approach promotes a well-performing, stable portfolio with a lower level of inherent risk. While delinquency and loss levels are factors in assessing the quantity of risk, examiners should give primary consideration to the standards and execution surrounding credit decisions.

There are many aspects of prudent underwriting, most of which are discussed in the *Consumer Compliance* booklets of the *Comptroller's Handbook*, including "Fair Lending." Prudent underwriting also is discussed in product-specific, retail lending-related booklets of the *Comptroller's Handbook*,[28] including "Residential Real Estate Lending," "Credit Card Lending," "Installment Lending," and "Student Lending."[29] Still, observing how the bank approaches a few basic credit practices often helps examiners make initial assessments of inherent risk levels. These practices include

- information verification practices.
- capacity-to-repay evaluations.
- debt burden considerations.
- approach to collateral.

Information verification practices: Sufficient due diligence should support credit information before it is used. Information routinely verified directly by banks with lower inherent portfolio risk includes current employer, primary income (amount, frequency, and type), supplemental sources of income (source, amount, and likely recurrence), and the value of any collateral taken to secure the loan. Some data can be reasonably verified using credit

---

[28] The Equal Credit Opportunity Act prohibits discrimination in any aspect of the credit transaction. For more information on the OCC's expectations for compliance, examiners should refer to the "Fair Lending" booklet of the *Comptroller's Handbook*.

[29] These booklets discuss consumer laws and regulations that apply to specified products. In addition, Regulation Z prohibits a credit card issuer from opening a credit card account for a consumer under an open-end (not home secured) consumer credit plan or increasing any credit limit applicable to such account, unless the issuer considers the consumer's ability to make the requested minimum monthly payments under the terms of the account, based on the consumer's income or assets and current obligations. Refer to 12 CFR 1026.51, "Ability to Pay." Regulation Z also requires creditors to make a reasonable and good faith determination that a consumer has the ability to repay certain mortgage loans by considering and verifying specified underwriting factors, including debt-to-income ratios. Refer to 12 CFR 1026.43, "Minimum Standards for Transactions Secured by a Dwelling," and 12 CFR 1026.34(a)(4), "Prohibited Acts or Practices in Connection With High-Cost Mortgages." Further, 12 CFR 34.3(b) prohibits national banks from making real estate loans based predominantly on the bank's realization of the foreclosure or liquidation value of the collateral, without regard to a borrower's ability to repay the loan according to its terms.

reports (including other debt obligations), public records (bankruptcies, judgments, etc.), and personal information (name and address, Social Security number, etc.). Banks diligent in verifying critical information tend to have a lower quantity of risk. Banks relying on customer assertions rather than direct verifications face greater uncertainty, have a higher inherent risk profile, and should have enhanced risk management practices to compensate.

Ability-to-repay evaluations: Repayment ability evaluations consider whether the borrower has the financial ability to repay the loan in full according to its terms. Three important considerations for a prudent capacity analysis are level of income, expected reliability of the income, and level of expenses. Each should be a factor in the credit decision and the loan structure.[30] Banks that routinely and diligently consider each tend to have a lower quantity of risk.

Debt burden considerations: Most ability-to-repay evaluations focus on the debt-to-income ratio, which looks at debt obligations on a flow basis, based on income and monthly payments for each. A second consideration should be the total principal amount of debt in relation to a borrower's income or resources. This information is a separate but important consideration, since it is possible for borrowers to accumulate substantial amounts of debt relative to their income while still meeting the bank's monthly debt service requirements. Even when monthly payments may be within acceptable ranges, aggregate loan balances can be a burden on the borrower's financial health and can jeopardize full repayment. To address this concern, some banks establish a maximum level of debt in relation to total income. For example, the bank may specify that total loan balances, excluding home mortgage debt, should not exceed some percentage of the borrower's gross annual income. Other methods may also mitigate risk, but in general credit practices that include prudent consideration of aggregate debt levels lead to lower inherent risk.

Approach to collateral: Often, banks decide collateral is necessary as a secondary source of repayment for certain types of loans. For loans to finance purchases, typically the collateral is the item purchased with the loan, such as a vehicle, home, or other type of tangible property. Collateral can be an important risk mitigating factor, offsetting potential losses for the lender and providing lower pricing for borrowers. Collateral is often difficult or costly to repossess, however, so it should not replace willingness and financial capacity as primary decision factors, and banks should not make a loan solely because of a favorable collateral position. Examiners should consider whether banks rely too heavily on collateral to offset other credit weaknesses or support poor loan structures. Prudent collateral use can lower the quantity of risk, but excessive reliance can lead to collateral-dependent lending, and a vulnerable, higher-risk portfolio.

Risk Layering

Risk layering refers to the existence of several higher-risk characteristics in a loan or portfolio. For example, risk layering may exist in a 72-month auto loan, with a 110 percent LTV ratio, to a subprime borrower, using stated income. Each characteristic may be within

---

[30] For certain types of retail lending, there are specific ability-to-repay assessment requirements. For example, refer to the "Truth in Lending Act" booklet of the *Comptroller's Handbook.*

established policy guidelines, but the combination may still make the risk excessive. This assessment is especially true when these types of loans make up large portfolio concentrations. Risk layering often leads to credit issues when economic conditions change. Because heightened risk can exist even if all terms are within, but near to, assigned cutoffs, management should exercise additional diligence to identify and monitor the potential for risk layering. Some banks control this potential exposure using tiered criteria; for example, auto loans with LTV ratios less than 90 percent may have loan terms up to 72 months, while loans with LTV ratios greater than 90 percent are limited to 60-month terms. Examiners should consider risk layering when evaluating portfolio risk, and discuss with management how the bank assesses potential risk layering when setting credit criteria and designing credit risk monitoring reports. Banks that consciously identify and control risk layering are likely to have portfolios with lower inherent risk than those that manage exposure simply through individual credit criteria.

A Sound Approach to Credit Approvals

Choosing Products and Target Markets

Retail lending policies should identify the types of loans the bank is willing to accept. Examples might include personal loans, auto loans or leases, credit cards, student loans, and loans to individuals secured by their personal residences. Loan policies should also state the types of loans the bank is unwilling to make within the retail portfolio because of oversight costs, system limitations, required expertise, or other reasons. Examples might include loans for speculative purposes (e.g., margin loans), loans to finance start-up costs for a new business, loans to corporations or partnerships, or real estate loans for investment properties. Lending policies should define product criteria, such as down payment requirements, amortization schedules, required collateral, and other terms and conditions. Product terms for revolving products should include standards for minimum monthly payments, revolving period length, and whether principal payments should be required even during a revolving period.

Target markets include geographic areas, borrowers' credit profiles, and methods used to find new customers (e.g., mailing lists, credit bureaus, or brokers). Desired credit profile is an important consideration, and the bank may decide to pursue prime or nonprime borrowers, recognizing that differences exist within these broad categories. For example, nonprime borrowers with poor credit histories may represent a higher risk than those trying to establish credit for the first time. The data available for analyzing these two groups differ, as does the method of predicting future payment performance. Examiners should assess whether the bank's credit criteria and underwriting guidelines recognize and accommodate these and other target market choices, taking into account potential fair lending and other compliance risks.

A product test, or pilot program, is an important consideration for new, expanded, or significantly modified products. Before full rollout, testing should determine whether risk, consumer acceptance, and other key assumptions made during the planning process hold true or vary within acceptable ranges. The testing phase should be designed carefully to avoid potential fair lending or unfair or deceptive practices issues that may arise when specific categories of consumers are selected for different or preferential treatment. For example, consumers should receive appropriate disclosure of information to avoid potential unfair or deceptive practices. In addition, the testing phase should identify potential consumer compliance, fair lending, BSA compliance, or money laundering risks that may arise from full implementation of the new product. Well-run banks establish aggregate and individual test limits (e.g., new product channel tests cannot exceed 5 percent of loan originations at any point) to limit and control exposure to new or untested products. Discipline is important, as is resisting the urge to forgo thorough testing.

Testing programs should also include key performance measures for evaluating success. An important prerequisite for such testing is assurance that pertinent data to monitor and evaluate results are readily available and reliable. Testing also involves forecasting expected results to give the performance measures a base and context. As testing progresses, management should explain and investigate significant variances.

Establishing Underwriting Criteria

Underwriting criteria define how the bank decides who is eligible for credit. Most important are measures for considering a borrower's financial capacity and character. Because the bank has the most complete and current borrower information at the time of application, decisions made during the underwriting process are crucial to credit quality. This topic is a key examination area, and examiners should expect a disciplined and structured process.

Policies should define expectations for obtaining and assessing borrower information. Most banks use multiple sources, relying on credit bureau data for credit history and the loan application for income, housing, and employment information. Most retail lenders also use credit scores, which use credit bureau data to project the probability of future payment performance based on predictive characteristics and experience.[31]

The following three key factors generally determine creditworthiness for retail borrowers:

- A reliable source of recurring income.
- A history of responsible performance.
- Sufficient income or assets to repay the subject debt and all other current and prospective debt.

For retail credit, a borrower's job-related income is usually the main source of repayment. Operating procedures should specify how to consider the source, reliability, frequency, and probable continuity of income, at least through the term of the loan. Some borrowers rely on cash reserves or other assets for repayment, so banks should have defined methods for assessing these repayment sources as well.

---

[31] Refer to OCC Bulletin 2011-12, "Sound Practices for Model Risk Management: Supervisory Guidance on Model Risk Management," for prudent practices associated with the use and oversight of credit scoring models.

One critical aspect of credit underwriting is how to evaluate the borrower's capacity to repay. The objective is to assess whether the borrower can reasonably afford the proposed debt along with all other credit obligations he or she may have. A primary examination objective is to consider whether the bank employs a practical, methodical, and objective process that is likely to promote sound credit decisions over time. Banks use many approaches when considering capacity. The most common approaches include the following:

- **Minimum income:** Establishes a minimum dollar income to qualify for a specific credit product.
- **Disposable monthly income:** Attempts to determine an allowable residual amount after deducting total monthly debt service expenses from gross (or net) income.
- **Payment-to-income:** Considers the monthly payment for the subject debt as a percentage of monthly income. The objective is to evaluate whether a specific loan payment is within normal, prudent limits.
- **Total housing debt-to-income:** Considers all housing costs (e.g., mortgage, real estate taxes, home insurance, and association dues) as a percentage of gross monthly income.[32]
- **Monthly debt service-to-income:** Considers all monthly required debt service payments (e.g., car payments, housing payments, and other monthly payments) as a percentage of gross monthly income.
- **Total debt owed-to-income:** Compares the total principal amount of outstanding debt (auto loans, credit cards, installment loans, etc.) with total annual income.

The OCC has not set maximum debt service capacity limits or required measurement approaches. A bank's policies and operating procedures should define how and when each approach may be used, including whether any of the approaches may be used alone or must be part of a broader capacity evaluation. Examiners should expect each bank to have a credible approach that complies with any product-specific debt-to-income considerations (e.g., Regulation Z).[33] A credible analysis most often includes a full debt-to-income analysis as the baseline capacity measure, with other measures such as total debt burden, payment-to-income, and disposable income buffers as useful supplements.

Debt-to-income calculations are not overly complicated, but the execution can vary widely within and across banks (for example, in some banks capacity-to-repay formulas may differ among products such as credit cards, mortgages, and automobile loans). The following are common issues that should be addressed in lending policies, as they may result in inconsistent calculations:

---

[32] In some cases, a borrower's credit report shows no mortgage debt and the loan application does not list a monthly rent expense. In that case, the bank often either verifies that the borrower has no housing expense or uses a minimum rent estimate based on geography (e.g., $800 per month).

[33] In particular, Regulation Z requires creditors originating certain mortgage loans to make a reasonable and good faith determination that a borrower will have a reasonable ability to repay a covered transaction at or before consummation (12 CFR 1026.43). Banks have three options for complying with the ability-to-repay (ATR) rule. They may (1) comply with the general ATR standards, (2) refinance a "non-standard" mortgage into a "standard" mortgage, or (3) make a "qualified mortgage." Refer to 12 CFR 1026.43, and the "Residential Real Estate Lending" and "Truth in Lending Act" booklets of the *Comptroller's Handbook* for additional information on the covered transactions, ATR, and qualified mortgages.

- **Other income:** Banks' policies should specify how to treat income other than normal salary, including income from self-employment, investments, commissions, and bonuses, to promote consistent calculations. Consideration can vary, but banks that place less emphasis on demonstrated recurring cash flow patterns tend to need stronger offsetting risk management practices.

- **Debt obligations from credit bureau information:** Banks commonly obtain debt information from credit reports as part of the capacity analysis. Credit bureaus reliably identify debt owed, but monthly payment information is not always available. Most banks have business rules to estimate monthly payment amounts, for example, using 1.5 percent to 2.5 percent of the outstanding balance. Some banks also have rules for considering credit bureau debt, such as eliminating monthly payments when only a few payments remain, or incorporating payment estimates on deferred debt such as student loans. In general, the more assumptions necessary, the stronger the risk management practices that are needed to mitigate uncertainties.

- **Available debt under revolving lines:** Measuring debt service capacity can be difficult with revolving credit programs. Available balances are easily accessible, allowing borrowers to increase monthly obligations without requesting new credit. Banks typically consider unused lines in one of three ways: assume that at some point the borrower will use the full credit line; assume that a certain percentage of available debt will be drawn; or assume that the borrower will not use the potential debt. The first method is most conservative and minimizes surprises. The second can be effective but requires good data and analysis. The third is the most lenient and requires close monitoring and controls.

- **Variable rate debt:** Variable interest rates are common for revolving products, such as credit cards and HELOCs. A rise in interest rates typically means higher payments, possibly raising the borrower's monthly debt-to-income ratio from acceptable to risky, even if the borrower takes on no additional debt. Prudent capacity evaluations build potential interest rate adjustments into the debt service analysis, helping to control potential risk.[34] Banks that ignore potential interest rate changes should control exposure with other methods.

Banks also use loan structure, collateral, and guarantees to help mitigate credit risk, but credit decisions should still depend primarily on the strength of the borrower's repayment capacity. Collateral especially should not be a substitute for a comprehensive capacity assessment, nor does collateral compensate for insufficient information or evidence that a borrower's primary source of repayment cannot service the debt. In addition, bank management should recognize that collateral values are often market driven and subject to change, and values that were protective at loan origination can be insufficient in a forced liquidation. Specific policies should address the use of collateral, procedures for ongoing valuation, and processes to provide certainty that collateral liens are properly perfected and enforceable.

---

[34] Refer also to 12 CFR 1026.43(c)(5)(i), "Minimum Standards for Transactions Secured by a Dwelling," for requirements with respect to debt service analysis for adjustable rate mortgages. When assessing a consumer's ability to repay an adjustable rate mortgage, a creditor must consider the higher of the introductory interest rate or the fully indexed rate for loans under the general ability-to-repay standard.

Loan Pricing Considerations

Loan pricing is an important component of credit risk management. As banks migrate from a single price per product to risk-based pricing, their main challenge is often managing a balance between pricing for risk and responding to competitors' rates to maintain volume or growth. Pricing errors can jeopardize portfolio performance and profitability, whether the bank purposefully or inadvertently prices above or below the market. Problems with pricing above the market include the following:

- **Lower-than-expected response rates:** When fewer consumers accept new loans, banks face higher acquisition costs per account as well as less ongoing product revenue. This result raises issues regarding whether revenue is sufficient to support the associated infrastructure and has potential implications for earnings and capital.
- **Adverse selection:**[35] Mispriced loans may inadvertently attract disproportionate volumes of the least creditworthy individuals. This happens because lower-risk customers take advantage of less costly financing options, and higher-risk customers tend to apply for and accept credit at almost any rate.
- **Higher-than-expected prepayment or attrition[36] rates:** If pricing and other terms are viewed as onerous, borrowers choose to pay off their loans as soon as possible or refinance them with lenders that offer more favorable terms. This phenomenon is known as "voluntary attrition" and is closely watched and managed in well-run banks.

Management sometimes chooses to price below the market in pursuit of growth. This pricing may have unintended consequences, and management's analysis should include realistic assessments of the level of risk being assumed. Potential negative consequences include the following:

- **Higher-than-expected response rates:** Unexpected loan application volumes can overwhelm the bank's ability to process applications efficiently and effectively. Beyond the potential for loss of business and significant operational problems, this may result in compliance issues[37] or increased liquidity risk from higher-than-anticipated funding needs.
- **Unrealizable or unsustainable profitability:** In general, market-rate pricing assumes a certain level of costs and a reasonable return. If response rates significantly exceed expectations (resulting in higher funding and operational costs) or performance falls below projections (resulting in higher collection expenses and credit losses), profitability

---

[35] Adverse selection refers to a disproportionately high response or acceptance rate to a marketing offer by high-risk customers in a targeted population. This situation generally occurs because the product or promotional design is flawed.

[36] Attrition refers to the closing of accounts either by the customer or the bank. The term is most commonly associated with credit card accounts.

[37] For instance, 12 CFR 202, "Equal Credit Opportunity Act" (Regulation B), requires that the creditor provide notice of action taken within a specific period (e.g., 30 days after taking adverse action). Refer to 12 CFR 1002.9(a), "Notifications."

can be jeopardized. Pricing below the market leaves the bank more vulnerable to unrealistic or unsustainable profitability.

- **Difficulties managing geographic or market expansion:** Expanding outside of established markets requires a level of control that may go beyond the bank's resources and management expertise. Difficulties may arise from inadequate knowledge of new geographic markets, adverse selection from brokers or dealers in newer markets, or operational risk considerations such as difficulties with handling repossessions when collateral is outside of the bank's normal local markets.[38]

When pricing for growth, forecasts should stratify expected revenue and anticipated loss rates by credit grade or credit score so expectations can be established regarding profitable performance. Bank forecasts should also include realistic assumptions for account retention, as well as the longer-term impact on profitability. Most introductory pricing strategies are loss leaders, and banks have difficulty achieving or sustaining profitability at those rates. Further, if strategies are not well-conceived with carefully constructed underwriting parameters, the bank may end up with a portfolio that consists of higher-risk borrowers locked into unrealistically low interest rates in terms of the credit risk posed. If the bank elects to offer low introductory rates, careful planning and forecasting are necessary to avoid problems. Banks should specifically consider the target markets and longer-term objectives, and design pricing initiatives accordingly.

Managing Loan Acquisition Sources

For retail lending, the various avenues for acquiring new borrowers or loan applications are known as marketing channels. While channels refer to the type of acquisition technique, marketing also extends to methods of identifying or pre-qualifying applicants, as well as the different levels of information required on the part of the applicants. As with other variables, the type of marketing used may result in different levels of credit and other risks.

Viewed in isolation, the least risky channel is a direct, full application from a borrower to a bank's loan officer. In this case, the loan officer has a complete summary of the applicant's financial condition, as well as the benefit of face-to-face interaction. As the channels become further removed from direct contact, and as the information obtained directly from the applicant decreases, the level of risk tends to rise.

As the scope and breadth of retail lending expands, loan origination has moved beyond sourcing loans through a bank's own offices and branches. For most banks, the use of indirect marketing channels is common, including the following:

- **Brokers:** Third parties that solicit applicants for various loan products, primarily real estate-related, and then "shop" the applications to several different lenders. The financial information provided is reasonably complete, and broker compensation varies but is typically based on the principal amount of each loan.

---

[38] Expanding into new markets can also raise potential fair lending risks. Refer to the "Fair Lending" booklet of the *Comptroller's Handbook* for additional information and discussion.

- **Dealers:** Third-party retailers that generate loan applications to facilitate sales of their products, generally automobiles, boats, recreational vehicles, pools, and spas. As with brokers, dealers often maintain relationships with several banks to obtain funding for even the least creditworthy consumers. Dealer compensation varies based on the bank's agreement with the individual dealer and the terms of the individual loan.

- **Correspondents:** Organizations that have agreements with one or more wholesale lenders to act as their retail representative, lending directly to consumers. Correspondent lenders generally use wholesale guidelines to approve and close loans with their own funds, and agree to buy back loans that deviate from wholesaler standards.

- **Internet:** Use of a bank-controlled Internet site or participation with an Internet loan broker or other third party to generate electronic applications. These applications may be bank-specific or may be forwarded to a number of lenders in a broker-type situation. The extent of the information requested varies based on the product involved and the third party, and may result in a subsequent request for additional information once the consumer has expressed interest in a product or group of products. Online data security and effective fraud controls are imperative for this channel. Fees for broker-originated applications or expressions of interest vary.

- **Marketplace lenders:** Generally, marketplace lending refers to the segment of the financial services industry that predominantly uses investment capital, nontraditional underwriting, and online platforms to lend to consumers and small businesses. Marketplace lenders may offer a wide variety of financial products, including small business loans, consumer loans, student loans, and real estate loans. Marketplace lenders may fund their loans through various means, including equity capital, commercial lines of credit, sale of whole loans to institutional investors, securitizations, and pass-through note programs.

Loans sourced in any of these ways help minimize overhead expenses but increase the need for robust quality assurance and third-party management functions. Arrangements with brokers, dealers, or other third-party sources should include adequate due diligence and well-structured agreements that describe factors such as quality and volume expectations, target acceptance rates, and compensation parameters.[39]

Another option for growth is through portfolio acquisition, i.e., purchasing an entire retail credit portfolio, a product portfolio, or any target segment from another institution. For large purchases, quality and performance are typically evaluated on a portfolio, rather than a loan-by-loan, basis. Comprehensive and effective due diligence (including account sampling) is critical for the bank to understand the level of risk assumed and price its offer appropriately.

As banks expand into new channels, examiners should consider whether systems can adequately manage and monitor activity from the new sources. Lack of product experience

---

[39] Refer to OCC Bulletin 2013-29, "Third-Party Relationships: Risk Management Guidance," for more information about third-party due diligence and management practices. Refer to 12 CFR 1026.36, "Prohibited Acts or Practices and Certain Requirements for Credit Secured by a Dwelling," for more information about permissible compensation for mortgage loan originators (including brokers) in connection with closed-end mortgage loans.

and the failure to implement a proper monitoring and control environment can lead to problems, including unexpected application volumes, compliance issues, application fraud, and other situations not contemplated in the planning process. The OCC supports responsible innovation[40] in retail lending, including the use of new or improved products, services, and processes that meet the evolving needs of consumers. Examiners should consider whether loan acquisition sources, including new or innovative channels, are approached responsibly, encourage fair access to financial services, and are managed in a manner that is consistent with sound risk management and protective of consumer rights.

Establishing Credit Approval Processes

Given the large loan volumes, retail lenders often attempt to automate as much of the credit approval process as possible. When practical, applications are often directed through rule-based criteria concerning profitability, credit standards, credit amounts, policy exceptions, and pricing. The objective is one of four main results:

- Auto-approve
- Auto-decline
- Recommended approve
- Recommended decline

Most decisions for unsecured loans fall into the auto-approve and auto-decline categories, since the underwriting criteria mainly consist of prior credit performance and some income-based capacity and loan amount standards. The recommended approve and recommended decline options generally flow to a bank staff member for manual underwriting.[41] Secured loans usually have some manual review and consideration of collateral values, advance rates, etc., but standard rules and decision criteria govern these aspects as well. For cost and efficiency reasons, bank management generally prefers to route as many applications as possible through the automated options to leverage technology and economies of scale. This makes the criteria at each decision point extremely important, and there should be policies regarding the support needed for each. Decision criteria for auto approvals and manual reviews should comply with the bank's written guidelines and should be approved by the appropriate level of management according to internal policy delegations. Additionally, a clear audit trail should document the approval process.

Prudent management of automated credit approval processes should include allocating sufficient resources to efficiently handle anticipated volumes, meet competitive processing

---

[40] The OCC defines responsible innovation as the use of new or improved financial products, services, and processes to meet the evolving needs of consumers, businesses, and communities in a manner consistent with sound risk management and aligned with the bank's overall business strategy. Visit the OCC's website at www.occ.gov for more information on responsible innovation.

[41] Examiners should also evaluate whether credit decisions made during these manual reviews are supported by prudent business processes and controls designed to manage potential fair lending and other compliance risks. These controls should include adequate monitoring reports, as well as periodic process and transaction reviews by independent control functions such as internal audit, risk management, or compliance management.

and pricing turnaround times, and make sound credit decisions consistent with the bank's credit strategies. Banks should have appropriate policies, procedures, and processes to ensure compliance with relevant laws and regulations, including the provision of required disclosures and notice to the customer regarding the credit decision.[42]

Sometimes, a single borrower may approach several different areas of the bank for various forms of credit (e.g., credit cards, mortgages, and auto loans). Banks may assign responsibilities in different ways, but when possible the credit granting process should coordinate the efforts of all relevant departments to ensure that credit extensions are coordinated and consistent, and that sound credit decisions are made.

Prudent Credit Administration

Credit administration refers to activities occurring once the credit decision is made. For retail credit portfolios, this includes actions related to account management, collections, risk identification, and portfolio management. Most of these actions relate to maintaining borrower and transaction information, monitoring individual and portfolio credit quality, monitoring loan agreement terms, handling borrower contact and correspondence, and, when necessary, executing collection actions.

Key risk management aspects of a well-run credit administration function include the following:

- **Efficient operations:** Efficient processes should exist for documentation follow-up, contractual monitoring, managing legal and compliance obligations, and managing and monitoring collateral.
- **Accurate and timely information:** Borrower and transaction information should be timely and processed efficiently into management information systems (MIS).
- **Prudent controls:** Effective internal controls should support all back-office processes.
- **Comprehensive compliance program:** Internal policies and procedures should address compliance with all applicable laws and regulations, and consistency with regulatory guidance.

The credit administration function will vary with the bank's size, complexity, risk profile, and organizational structure. In large banks, specific credit administration responsibilities are often assigned to specialized departments that have the expertise and economies of scale to handle high-volume operations. In community banks, a few individuals may handle multiple functions, so rotating duties and maintaining sound internal controls are key to effectively managing the risks. When credit administration staff performs sensitive functions,[43] the staff should report to managers independent of the credit origination and approval process.

---

[42] Refer to footnote 5.

[43] Sensitive functions generally include those in which a person has influence over financial records and access to assets; in which a significant error would result in the inaccurate reporting of transactions; or in which false information could allow a person to gain control of assets.

Sensitive functions may include custody of key documents, wiring out funds, or entering contract terms and credit limits into servicing systems.

One important credit administration responsibility is appropriate control of credit and collateral documentation. Credit documentation should include all the information used to make the original credit decision, as well as sufficient information to track subsequent decisions and the history of the credit. For example, retail credit documentation should include the initial application, borrower financial information, credit assessment information, internal memorandums, and records of any customer contact. Collateral documentation, if applicable, should include initial valuations, refreshed values, lien perfections, and insurance information. The loan review function should include credit and collateral documentation reviews as part of its normal scope to determine whether credit and collateral documentation is complete and all loan approvals and other necessary documents are obtained.

Managing Retail Accounts

For a retail lender, account management objectives are generally to enhance borrower performance, maximize profitability, and manage attrition as efficiently and effectively as possible. Account management programs can target individual accounts or large portfolio segments, and the strategies can be manual or automated. Analyzing borrower behavior and performance provides useful insight into potential exposures and opportunities to manage risk and increase profitability. Relevant data come from customer files; automated tools, such as behavioral and credit bureau scoring; and other management reports.

Account management strategies often involve credit decisions such as line increases and decreases, freeze programs, and over-limit authorizations. These types of actions pose credit risk and should be as controlled as the initial underwriting decision. Account management programs often require substantial involvement from marketing, customer service, customer retention, and operations, and may also include input from control functions such as risk management, compliance, quality assurance, and audit.

In many community banks, account management is less formal, often conducted only after a customer request or question. Large banks are more likely to actively manage accounts by, for example, targeting portfolio segments proactively to respond to economic conditions or competition. Regardless of bank size, the basic approach should be similar: the range of available account management activities should be established in advance, policies and operating procedures should guide actions, and management reporting should monitor the performance, profitability, and risk characteristics of accounts subject to account management activities.[44]

---

[44] Bank management should maintain policies that ensure consistent treatment of similarly situated customers in over-limit decisions (and other account decisions discussed in this booklet, e.g., approvals and line increases) to avoid violating fair lending and other consumer protection laws. Additionally, bank management should maintain policies that address the Fair Housing Act (42 USC 3605), the Equal Credit Opportunity Act (15 USC 1691), section 5 of the Federal Trade Commission Act, which prohibits unfair or deceptive acts or practices, and section 1036 of the Consumer Financial Protection Act, which prohibits unfair, deceptive, or abusive acts or practices.

Common account management activities with credit risk implications include the following:

- **Credit line management:** As with assigning initial credit lines, criteria for credit line increases should focus on the repayment capacity of the borrower. When poorly managed, practices such as offering large credit limits as a marketing tool or liberally increasing credit lines to promote customer retention, increase the risk profile of individual borrowers and the portfolio as a whole. In general, credit lines should be increased only for accountholders demonstrating the financial capacity to perform at the new, higher credit limit.[45] As a prudent practice, banks should have defined standards for all significant credit line increase programs. Community banks without formal credit line increase programs should still maintain prudent guidelines for line increases.

- **Over-limit approvals:** Most banks establish explicit credit limits based on the borrower's financial condition and repayment capacity at a given point in time. When a borrower requests amounts above his or her established credit limit, the bank must decide whether additional credit is warranted. Over-limit approvals increase risk and should be closely managed. In general, over-limit approvals should be granted under established parameters, and only to customers who are paying as agreed under their current terms. Reporting should allow management to effectively monitor and control over-limit activity, including the subsequent performance of accounts for which over-limit advances were approved. Over-limit approval standards should be established in advance, with specific criteria defined for qualification, amounts, and repayment. Account management practices that do not adequately control authorizations and provide for timely repayment (typically at the next billing cycle, but generally no longer than three to six months) significantly increase the credit risk profile of the borrower and portfolio.

- **Account closures:** Although account closures are frequent for delinquent accounts, there may be other circumstances under which current accounts should be closed as another facet of controlling risk, contingent liabilities, and costs. For example, in addition to closing accounts of deceased and bankrupt accountholders, it may be prudent to close accounts that have been inactive for a specified period, or those with accountholders that have exhibited significant credit score deterioration over a relatively short time.[46]

---

[45] The Credit Card Accountability Responsibility and Disclosure Act of 2009 requires credit card issuers to assess a customer's ability to make the required minimum periodic payments under the terms of the account based on the customer's income or assets and current obligations. Refer to 12 CFR 1026.51, "Ability to Pay," and the "Truth in Lending Act" booklet of the *Comptroller's Handbook* for information on ability-to-repay requirements and guidance.

[46] Regulation Z provides limitations on when a HELOC account can be terminated, suspended, or reduced. Refer to 12 CFR 1026.40(f), "Limitations on Home Equity Plans." For example, the bank can freeze or reduce a credit line only under a limited set of circumstances, including during any period in which (1) the value of the collateral declines significantly below the appraised value for the purposes of the HELOC; (2) the consumer is in default of a material obligation under the loan agreement; or (3) the bank reasonably believes the consumer will be unable to fulfill the repayment obligations under the plan because of a material deterioration in the borrower's financial circumstances.

Additionally, the Consumer Financial Protection Bureau amended its mortgage servicing rules in October 2016, adding provisions defining who is a successor in interest and detailing the treatment of successors in interest and consumers in bankruptcy with respect to periodic statements and the servicing of delinquent first lien

- **Retention strategies:** The retail credit market is extremely competitive with constant substitute offers and refinancing opportunities. Consequently, many banks actively attempt to identify profitable loan customers likely to be targeted by competing offers and proactively offer them more attractive or enhanced products. These offers typically include reduced interest rates, higher credit lines, convenience checks, or upgrades to associated products or services. Even banks not engaging in proactive contact generally develop customer profitability and performance guidelines triggering product offers or refinancing if a customer calls to close an account or request a pay-off. As with other account management activities, banks with larger or more complex retail portfolios should monitor and analyze the volume of retention calls (in and out), the acceptance rate, and the ongoing performance of accounts accepting retention offers. This information is critical to assess the profitability of retention initiatives and to adjust practices as necessary.

- **Early customer outreach programs:** Active borrower outreach can be an effective account management practice and is most prevalent for loans such as home mortgages,[47] HELOCs, automobile loans, and automobile leasing programs. For HELOCs, the end-of-draw period[48] often results in substantially higher amortization payments and a loss of utility once the line access ends. Prudent lenders reach out to borrowers well before their scheduled line termination dates to establish contact, obtain information, and engage the borrowers in discussions regarding potential repayment options. For auto leasing, banks typically contact customers before lease-end to determine whether the customers plan to return or purchase the vehicle. In either case, outreach activities often begin well in advance of significant event dates, sometimes up to 12 months in advance. Borrower outreach is also common for subprime lenders that call borrowers to verify payment terms and remind them of upcoming payments. Early outreach programs can be effective in mitigating credit risk exposure, and examiners should expect sound, practical research and analysis supporting the timing and terms of any outreach programs used.

- **Extensions and renewals:** Bank policies typically include guidelines for when loans can be extended or renewed, and any fees involved. The interagency "Uniform Classification and Account Management Policy"[49] states these activities should be reasonable in terms of frequency, duration, and creditworthiness requirements. Generally, extensions and renewals should be controlled and based on an updated evaluation of the borrower's willingness and ability to repay. Management should track the volumes involved, monitor

---

mortgage loans. The mortgage servicing rules become effective in October 2017 or April 2018, depending on the provision. Refer to 81 Fed. Reg. 72160 (final rule) and 71977 (interpretations), October 19, 2016.

[47] Refer to 12 CFR 1024.39, "Early Intervention Requirements for Certain Borrowers," regarding requirements under Regulation X for federally related mortgage loans.

[48] Refer to OCC Bulletin 2014-29, "Risk Management of Home Equity Lines of Credit Approaching the End-of-Draw Periods: Interagency Guidance," regarding regulatory expectations for management oversight of HELOCs approaching their end-of-draw period.

[49] Refer to OCC Bulletin 2000-20, "Uniform Retail Credit Classification and Account Management Policy: Policy Implementation."

subsequent performance of accounts extended or renewed, and use the information to develop and update terms and standards around these actions.

- **Payment holidays or "skip-a-pay":** A payment holiday refers to the practice of allowing a performing borrower to skip a payment for a month. Most often, the bank picks the payment-free month, but sometimes borrowers are allowed to choose. This practice has evolved in response to competition, and should be very carefully controlled. Although this practice can be popular with borrowers, and is generally profitable for the bank in that interest continues to accrue and the loan term is lengthened, it clouds risk analyses relying on regular payment streams. If offered, payment holidays should be in conformance with applicable law, controlled, and available only to the most creditworthy customers.

- **Pay-aheads:** Pay-aheads occur when a customer makes a payment exceeding the minimum amount due. To the extent permitted by law,[50] rather than applying the excess amount to the loan's principal balance and reducing the number of payments remaining, the bank may apply the excess to subsequent payments. The result is that the customer is not required to make another payment until the excess amount is exhausted. Pay-aheads may be used in a controlled manner for installment credit, but are generally inappropriate for revolving credit, because they have the potential to mask or distort useful early warning signs like early-stage delinquencies. Banks accepting payments above the minimum due on credit card accounts must comply with 12 CFR 1026.53, "Allocation of Payments," which sets forth allocation requirements for excess payment amounts.

Handled prudently, account management activities can benefit both the lender and the borrower. Active account management helps prevent attrition and can increase profitability. As with any credit activity, however, poorly conceived or executed actions can significantly increase risk. To manage risk, lenders should actively manage both the types and timing of account management actions to avoid over-lending or over-leveraging customers. Management should have reports and analyses to accurately monitor activities and identify and explain performance trends or anomalies in a timely manner. Examiners should consider how management uses this information to adjust policies and strategies, and how promptly management responds to emerging issues. In general, the better management understands the bank's risk profile, products, and customer bases, the more effective the bank's account management practices will be.

Collecting Delinquent Accounts

The collection function manages the bank's problem accounts. Managing risk and minimizing losses require skilled staff, sound policies that are consistent with applicable laws

---

[50] Various provisions of Regulation Z address payment application depending on the underlying credit type. Refer to 12 CFR 1026.32(c), "Requirements for High-Cost Mortgages" (principal-dwelling closed-end mortgage); 12 CFR 1026.41(d)(5), "Periodic Statements for Residential Mortgage Loans" (closed-end mortgages generally); and 12 CFR 1026.10, "Payments" (open-end account).

and regulations,[51] and well-conceived strategies. Orderly repayment is the goal, with repossession, foreclosure, or other legal action a last resort.

Collections policies should provide comprehensive guidance for staff, addressing the full range of collections activities, with particular attention on the following:

- **Authority levels:** Including limits with respect to making payment, forbearance, concession, or forgiveness arrangements with borrowers. Policies should establish review and approval parameters and reporting requirements.
- **Collector compensation:** Including incentive payment programs and required compliance with policies, procedures, and all relevant laws and regulations. Examiners should determine that collector compensation programs appropriately balance the collection of accounts with efficiency standards. These programs should promote compliance with all collection laws and regulations.
- **Collector monitoring:** Describing in detail how collector performance is monitored and evaluated, including call monitoring programs and requirements.[52]

Staffing plans should reflect the number of collectors and level of expertise necessary to handle current and near-term projected collection volumes. In general, collection efforts are more effective when supported by experienced and stable management and staff. Overall productivity suffers as experience levels decrease or turnover increases, and severely understaffed units tend to show disproportionately poor results. In small community banks, loan officers may be responsible for collecting their own loans. As volumes increase, separate collection units are common, initially collecting all product types and then specializing at the largest operations. Some banks outsource some or all collections activities to third-party specialists. Such banks may, for example, handle early-stage delinquencies in house and transfer delinquent accounts to a third-party agency once the account becomes 90 days past due. Many different approaches can be effective as long as bank management recognizes that effective collections requires staff skills and experience that are consistent with the size, volume, and complexity of the bank's risk profile and the products offered.

Operational approaches vary in terms of prioritization, work queues, and the form and frequency of customer contact. Most banks prioritize collection accounts by delinquency level, dollars at risk, credit scores, or some combination of those factors. Collector tools include payment reminder calls, text messages, e-mails, statement notices, letters, telephone calls, legal action, and payment plans and workout programs. Collection strategies govern what actions collectors take at what point in the collection process, and the diligence to

---

[51] Among the laws and regulations that are relevant to a bank's collection function are the mortgage servicing requirements in 12 CFR 1024, "Real Estate Settlement Procedures Act (Regulation X)"; Servicemembers Civil Relief Act, 50 USC 3901, et seq.; section 5 of the Federal Trade Commission Act; 15 USC 45, "Unfair Methods of Competition Unlawful; Prevention by Commission"; and the Fair Debt Collection Practices Act, 15 USC 1692, et seq.

[52] Examiners should refer to product-specific retail lending booklets of the *Comptroller's Handbook* such as "Credit Card Lending," "Residential Real Estate Lending" and "Installment Lending" for discussions of the specific factors and types of reporting common in collection activities for individual products.

---

actively monitor collections and track the effectiveness of strategies is a key aspect of collections management and oversight.

Large collection units are constantly re-evaluating and revising strategies to improve contact rates and elicit the most cost-effective responses in terms of dollars collected and losses averted. Strategies typically vary based on borrowers' risk profiles, dollars at risk, and other variables. For example, strategies employed for subprime portfolios are often considerably more labor-intensive and active than those for the prime population. The bank's risk management area often works closely with the collection department to develop strategies, analyze results, and make modifications as warranted.

Collector productivity is also linked to the use of technology and the quality of initial and ongoing training. Collection technology typically includes using automated dialers and call optimization software that "remembers" the best time to call customers based on past successful contacts. Training should focus on the effective use of technology, building strong negotiation skills, and providing a comprehensive understanding of the bank's policies and the various federal and state legal requirements.

The following collection practices, among others, should be used judiciously because they can distort a portfolio's reported performance if used excessively or inappropriately:

- **Re-aging:** Returning an open-end account to current status without collecting the total amount of principal, interest, and fees that are contractually due.
- **Extensions:** Extending monthly payments on a closed-end loan and rolling the maturity back by the number of months extended.
- **Deferrals:** Deferring a contractually due payment on a closed-end loan without affecting other terms of the loan, including maturity. The account is shown current upon granting the deferral.
- **Renewals:** Underwriting a matured, closed-end loan generally at its outstanding principal amount and on similar terms.
- **Rewrites:** Underwriting an existing loan by significantly changing its terms, including payment amounts, interest rates, amortization schedules, or final maturity.

Re-aging of open-end accounts and extensions, deferrals, renewals, and rewrites of closed-end loans can be used to help borrowers overcome temporary financial difficulties, such as a job loss or medical emergency. A liberal policy on re-aging, extensions, deferrals, renewals, or rewrites can mask the true performance and delinquency status of portfolios. Prudent use is acceptable, however, when it is based on a renewed willingness and ability to repay the loan, and when it is structured and controlled in accordance with sound internal policies and operating procedures. Each of these practices is subject to the Federal Financial Institutions Examination Council's (FFIEC) Uniform Retail Credit Classification and Account

Management Policy[53] standards, including ongoing monitoring and adequate documentation for each practice.

The use and structure of workout and forbearance programs also require prudent management.[54] Payment terms for workout and forbearance programs should predominantly include principal amortization and specifically prohibit negative amortization.[55] Generally, interest should not be capitalized when the creditworthiness of the borrower is in question.[56] The end result should be a loan structure with a reasonable payment plan that the borrower can sustain based on the circumstances of his or her hardship. Evidence of poorly structured or poorly managed workout and forbearance programs include liberal repayment terms with extended amortization periods, high charge-off rates, migration of accounts from one workout program to another, multiple re-ages or extensions, and poor monitoring of program performance. Examiners should be critical of workout programs that are not managed properly, and require the bank to take appropriate corrective action. These actions may include adversely classifying entire segments of portfolios, placing loans on nonaccrual, increasing loan-loss reserves, and directing charge-offs to appropriately recognize losses. Examiners should be especially alert to workout programs that are used to defer losses or delay problem loan recognition, and require corrective action when identified.

Monitoring Portfolio Quality

Retail credit portfolios can generate substantial credit risk for the bank, although the exposure generally has a different dynamic compared with commercial portfolios. Retail exposures are typically numerous, but relatively small, and default by any single borrower seldom threatens the bank's solvency. This inherent diversity aids in concentration management, but also makes retail portfolios susceptible to broad economic issues such as

---

[53] Refer to OCC Bulletin 2000-20, "Uniform Retail Credit Classification and Account Management Policy: Policy Implementation."

[54] Workout and forbearance programs generally refer to agreements in which the balance owed is placed on a fixed (dollar or percentage) repayment schedule in accordance with modified, concessionary terms and conditions, generally in lieu of foreclosure or other legal action. The repayment terms typically require amortization or liquidation of the balance owed over a defined payment period. These arrangements are often used when a customer is unable to repay the loan in accordance with its original terms, but shows the willingness and ability to repay the loan in accordance with its modified terms and conditions. Refer to OCC Bulletin 2000-20, "Uniform Retail Credit Classification and Account Management Policy: Policy Implementation," and OCC Bulletin 2003-1, "Credit Card Lending: Account Management and Loss Allowance Guidance," for additional regulatory guidance on the prudent use, control, and oversight of workout and forbearance programs.

[55] Some banks also use temporary hardship programs that help borrowers overcome temporary financial difficulties, but these are generally short term (less than 12 months) and may not always include principal amortization. Any such programs should be offered in conformance with applicable law.

[56] Other considerations about the appropriateness of interest capitalization are whether it was included in the original loan terms to compensate for a planned temporary lack of borrower cash flow, and whether similar loan terms can be obtained from other lenders. Any capitalization of interest should follow generally accepted accounting principles and the FFIEC's "Instructions for Preparation of Consolidated Reports of Condition and Income."

---

employment levels, general interest rate changes, and other systemic conditions. It also allows retail lenders to better estimate default levels and manage losses, affording the opportunity to build loss rates more reliably into loan pricing.

A second key characteristic of retail loans is that, absent fraud, losses tend to follow consistent patterns. For example, borrowers typically fail to make a minimum monthly payment or rapidly increase the use of a credit card line in the initial stages of a troubled situation. This pattern makes warning signs such as early-stage delinquencies and rising utilization rates important credit quality signals that should be monitored closely. It also underscores the importance of required minimum payments that allow borrowers to demonstrate capacity through performance each month. Further, diligent monitoring allows retail lenders to proactively manage portfolio-level risk by adjusting marketing approaches, increasing minimum credit scores, or changing pricing to enhance cash flow buffers.

Rapid portfolio growth also has the potential to distort portfolio performance and credit quality measures. Because of this potential, in addition to monitoring delinquencies and charge-off trends, management should also monitor performance using analytical techniques that consider the effects of growth. The two most common are vintage analysis and lagged analysis.

- **Vintage analysis:** Grouping for analysis loans that were made in a given time frame. For example, management may evaluate performance of all new car loans made in 2012, and compare them with performance of new car loans in other years (or "vintages") to evaluate how underwriting or decision criteria may have affected performance.
- **Lagged analysis:** Adjusting the denominator in a loss rate (or delinquency rate) ratio to minimize the effects of growth or attrition. In a lagged analysis, management may compare a given month's charge-offs (or delinquencies) with the outstanding balances from an earlier period, e.g., six months prior. The underlying assumption is that a fast-growing (or rapidly declining) portfolio tends to distort reported loss rates.[57]

Both approaches help adjust for the effect of portfolio growth or contraction, and management at banks of all sizes should consider them when portfolio balances are changing rapidly.

A third important portfolio-level issue involves identifying and managing credit concentrations.[58] Concentrations take many forms and pose risk whenever a significant number of credits tend to be influenced by a few key factors. For example, although generally diversified, retail portfolio performance tends to react positively and negatively to

---

[57] For example, if a bank uses a 180-day delinquency period for charge-offs, absent fraud or other early charge-off actions, it will take six months for a problem account to migrate through the delinquency buckets. If at the same time the outstanding loans in the denominator are growing, the combination of growth and charge-off delays tends to understate reported loss rates. The opposite effect occurs in a shrinking portfolio, where a failure to "lag" the denominator (outstanding loans) tends to overstate loss rates.

[58] Refer to OCC Bulletin 1999-38, "Interagency Guidelines for Real Estate Lending Policies: Treatment of High LTV Residential Real Estate Loans," for a discussion of the monitoring, reporting, and concentration limits associated with high LTV residential mortgage loans.

broad economic factors, such as unemployment, interest rates, and housing prices. During a recession, rising unemployment often contributes to higher default rates from income interruptions, while at the same time housing prices—and collateral values—fall because of reduced demand. If deep and widespread enough, the factors can feed on each other, worsening the cycle and resulting in unexpected, broad portfolio deterioration.

To manage exposure to retail credit concentrations, many banks use active management of concentration and risk limits as part of their risk management framework. Concentration and risk limits set upper bounds on exposures to limit the potential for unexpected events to impair the bank's earnings or solvency.[59] Limits can be either specific values (loan or commitment amounts) or linked to other measures, such as growth rates, portfolio mix, market share, or capital. Concentration limits are usually established as a percentage of capital, whereas risk limits may be expressed as a percentage of assets, percentage of loans, a growth rate, or other relevant measure.

The approach to setting limits varies among banks, but generally occurs at three main levels, the overall portfolio, individual products, and individual product segments or geographic areas. Higher-risk products and segments generally have lower limits, and banks should consider factors such as economic conditions, management expertise, and the results of stress tests[60] when setting prudent levels. Active limit management is an important risk management tool, and limits should be set at meaningful levels—not so high that they are never approached, but not so low that they will be breached constantly. Examiners should recognize that banks limited by geography, strategy, or expertise cannot always easily diversify, but that does not exempt banks from the need to actively manage and monitor exposures against prudent risk limits.

Limit monitoring should include regular reports that compare positions with projections or established thresholds. Exceptions to limits should be rare and typically include a requirement to reduce exposures or escalate the issue to the board or designated oversight committee as exposure levels approach a breach. Many banks set limits at two levels to facilitate monitoring and oversight, a hard limit and a threshold limit. Hard limits are seldom breached, while threshold limits trigger active dialogue and an action plan when reached. Limit monitoring and exception approvals should be performed outside the business line, typically by a risk management function or other independent control group. Loans that approach threshold or hard limits should prompt senior-management discussions about the nature of the underlying exposure, the economic outlook for the segment, region, or sector, and possible alternatives to controlling exposure levels, up to and including a temporary limit increase or the need to curtail a position. Oversight committees should approve any limit increase before a request to the board or other senior risk committee occurs. Examiners

---

[59] Refer to the "Concentrations of Credit" booklet of the *Comptroller's Handbook* for more information on identifying and managing risks associated with concentrations of credit.

[60] Refer to OCC Bulletin 2012-14, "Stress Testing: Interagency Stress Testing Guidance"; OCC Bulletin 2012-33, "Community Bank Stress Testing: Supervisory Guidance"; and OCC Bulletin 2012-41, "Stress Testing: Final Rule for Dodd–Frank Act Section 165(i)," for supervisory guidance on the use of stress testing to identify and quantify risk in loan portfolios and establish effective strategic and capital planning processes.

should expect committee minutes to document the level and depth of discussions, including decisions reached and any follow-up expected of the business line.

Banks should have a defined process for setting and considering limit changes, including appropriate analysis and support as well as designated approval authorities. In community banks, the board or a designated board committee typically monitors exposures rather than limits and approves any changes to limits.

Heightened Standards

The risk governance framework should include concentration and risk limits and, as applicable, front line unit risk limits, for the relevant risks. Concentration and front line unit risk limits should limit excessive risk taking and, when aggregated across such units, provide that these risks do not exceed the limits established in the covered bank's risk appetite statement.[61]

In some cases, the bank's trade area, geographic location, or lack of access to economically diverse borrowers may make avoiding or reducing concentrations difficult. In others, the bank may accept concentrations to capitalize on expertise in a particular industry or economic sector. Often bank management determines that the bank is adequately compensated for incurring certain exposures and assumes some level of concentration risk deliberately.

Even when intentionally assuming concentrations, bank management should actively monitor and manage exposures, including making use of alternatives to reduce or mitigate concentration levels. Mitigation can include pricing for the additional risk, increased holdings of capital, or using loan sales and securitization to diversify exposures.

As in most areas, effectiveness of the bank's portfolio monitoring depends largely on the quality of management reporting. The content and design of management reports should enable the board and all levels of management to identify and manage exposures, as well as determine whether appropriate levels of capital and reserves exist to mitigate the risks. The quality, detail, and timeliness of management reporting are critical. Simple and direct reports should support the monitoring of exposures against established limits and promote the active management of portfolios or segments approaching established thresholds. In particular, business line and risk managers tailor the information to the complexity of the business and the composition and quality of the subject portfolios. The entire reporting process should also fall within the scope of independent review functions, such as credit policy, loan review, and internal audit.

Critical Reviews of Pricing and Profitability

One important internal risk management exercise is the diligent analysis of revenues, profits, and losses. This analysis should occur for the retail business as a whole, and for each major product. Strong managers constantly challenge forecasts and assumptions, attempting to

---

[61] For more information, refer to 12 CFR 30, appendix D, II.F, "Concentration and Front Line Unit Risk Limits."

understand strengths, opportunities, and vulnerabilities inherent in their business models. Studying cash flows and the impact on profits is vital to knowing whether the risks assumed are producing the returns expected. This analysis should focus on exactly how cash flows in and out of the business. Each significant revenue and expense line item should be evaluated at a point in time, on a trend basis, and compared with projections, budgets, or expectations. The objective is to understand the contribution, importance, and sustainability of each revenue and expense line item to better understand the strengths and vulnerabilities of the business model.

Some small, non-complex community banks may perform this type of analysis through their budget variance process. Large banks often expand the analysis to the business line and significant segment levels to consider product and target market decisions, as well as the practical effects of competition. Careful analysis helps management understand the implications of pricing and funding choices, improving the chances that higher-risk products produce higher returns and that unprofitable products or product segments are curtailed.

At the most complex banks, management typically extends the analysis to the vintage or sub-product segment, by source, product structure, credit score range, or other defining characteristic. This level of analysis provides a better conceptual understanding of how and where risk is assumed, how marketing and acquisition choices affect cash flows, and how effectively resources are allocated. Each level of analysis serves as an important validation tool for the risk assessment process.

This same analytical discipline should apply when a product is highly profitable as when it loses money. Often, the same factors that cause losses—rapid expansion, mispricing, poorly designed loan structures, model error, etc.—may exist in a highly profitable product. When revenues are high, there is little pressure to analyze how the profitability occurs. This failure to question highly profitable segments may mask underlying problems until economic conditions change. Disciplined bank management questions profits as thoroughly as losses, primarily through a rigorous, systematic understanding of the true cash flows for each business.

Nonaccrual Status for Retail Loans

Banks should follow the FFIEC's "Instructions for Preparation of Consolidated Reports of Condition and Income" (call report instructions) when determining the accrual status for consumer loans. As a general rule, banks shall not accrue interest, amortize deferred net loan fees or costs, or accrete a discount on any asset if

- the asset is maintained on a cash basis because of deterioration in the financial condition of the borrower,
- payment in full of principal or interest is not expected, or

- principal or interest has been in default for a period of 90 days or more unless the asset is <u>both</u> well secured <u>and</u> in the process of collection.[62]

The call report instructions provide two exceptions to the general rule:[63]

(1) Consumer loans and loans secured by a one- to four-family residential property need not be placed in nonaccrual status when principal or interest is due and unpaid for 90 days or more. Nevertheless, consumer and one- to four-family residential property loans should be subject to other alternative methods of evaluation to assure that the bank's net income is not materially overstated. To the extent that the bank has elected to carry a consumer or one- to four-family residential property loan in nonaccrual status on its books, the loan must be reported as nonaccrual in the bank's call report.

(2) Purchased credit-impaired loans need not be placed in nonaccrual status when the criteria for accrual of income under the interest method specified in Accounting Standards Codification (ASC) Subtopic 310-30, "Receivables – Loans and Debt Securities Acquired with Deteriorated Credit Quality," are met, regardless of whether the loans had been maintained in nonaccrual status by the seller. For purchased credit-impaired loans with common risk characteristics that are aggregated and accounted for as a pool, the determination of nonaccrual or accrual status should be made at the pool level, not at the individual loan level.[64]

As a general rule, a loan in nonaccrual status may be restored to accrual status when

- none of its principal and interest is due and unpaid, and the bank expects repayment of the remaining contractual principal and interest, or
- it otherwise becomes well secured and is in the process of collection.

The OCC's *Bank Accounting Advisory Series* and the "Rating Credit Risk" booklet of the *Comptroller's Handbook* provide more information for recognizing nonaccrual loans, including the appropriate treatment of cash payments for loans in nonaccrual status.

---

[62] An asset is "well secured" if it is secured (1) by collateral in the form of liens on or pledges of real or personal property, including securities, that have a realizable value sufficient to discharge the debt (including accrued interest) in full, or (2) by the guarantee of a financially responsible party. An asset is "in the process of collection" if collection of the asset is proceeding in due course either (1) through legal action, including judgment enforcement procedures, or (2) in appropriate circumstances, through collection efforts not involving legal action that are reasonably expected to result in repayment of the debt or in its restoration to a current status in the near future.

[63] For more information, refer to the "Nonaccrual Status" entry in the "Glossary" section of the call report instructions. This entry describes the general rule for the accrual of interest, as well as exceptions for retail loans. The entry also describes criteria for returning a nonaccrual loan to accrual status.

[64] For more information, refer to the "Purchased Credit-Impaired Loans and Debt Securities" entry in the "Glossary" section of the call report instructions.

Risk Rating Retail Loans

OCC Bulletin 2000-20, "Uniform Retail Credit Classification and Account Management Policy: Policy Implementation" (classification policy), establishes standards for classifying retail credit for banks subject to OCC supervision.[65] This is broad policy guidance, adopted on an interagency basis to promote prudent and consistent treatment across financial institutions. In general, the federal banking agencies have recognized that a retail credit portfolio typically consists of a large number of relatively small-balance loans, so evaluating the quality of a retail credit portfolio on a loan-by-loan basis can be inefficient and burdensome. Therefore, the agencies have adopted a practical expedient for retail credit loan classification purposes based on individual borrower repayment performance. The classification policy states, in general, that troubled retail loans should be classified for regulatory purposes based on the following criteria:

- **Open- and closed-end retail loans past due 90 cumulative days** from the contractual due date should be classified substandard.
- **Closed-end retail loans past due 120 cumulative days and open-end retail loans past due 180 cumulative days** from the contractual due date should be classified loss and charged off.[66] In lieu of charging off the entire loan balance, loans with non-real estate collateral may be written down to the value of the collateral, less cost to sell, if repossession of collateral is assured and in process.
- **One- to four-family residential real estate loans and home equity loans past due 90 days** or more with LTV ratios greater than 60 percent should be classified substandard. Properly secured residential real estate loans with LTV ratios equal to or less than 60 percent are generally not classified based solely on delinquency status. Home equity loans to the same borrower at the same bank as the senior mortgage loan with a combined LTV ratio equal to or less than 60 percent need not be classified. Home equity loans for which the bank does not hold the senior mortgage and that are past due 90 days or more, however, should be classified substandard, even if the LTV ratio is equal to, or less than, 60 percent.
- **For open- and closed-end loans secured by residential real estate**, a current assessment of value should be made no later than when the loan reaches 180 days past due. Any outstanding loan balance in excess of the value of the property, less cost to sell, should be classified loss and charged off.

---

[65] The interagency classifications used for retail credit—substandard, doubtful, and loss—are defined in OCC Bulletin 2000-20, published at 65 Fed. Reg. 36903. The classification policy also states that although the OCC does not require institutions to adopt identical classification definitions, institutions should classify their assets using a system that can be easily reconciled with the regulatory classification system.

[66] For operational purposes, whenever a charge-off is necessary under this policy, it should be taken no longer than the end of the month in which the applicable time period elapses. Any full payment received after the 120- or 180-day charge-off threshold, but before month-end charge-off, may be considered in determining whether the charge-off remains appropriate. Open-end retail accounts that are placed on a fixed repayment schedule should follow the charge-off time frame for closed-end loans.

- **Loans in bankruptcy** should be classified loss and charged off within 60 days of receipt of notification of filing from the bankruptcy court or within the time frames specified in the classification policy, whichever is shorter, unless the bank can clearly demonstrate and document that repayment is likely to occur. Loans with collateral may be written down to the value of the collateral, less cost to sell. Any loan balance not charged off should be classified substandard until the borrower re-establishes the ability and willingness to repay for a period of at least six months.[67]
- **Fraudulent loans** should be classified loss and charged off no later than 90 days from discovery or within the time frames specified in the classification policy, whichever is shorter.
- **Loans of deceased persons** should be classified loss and charged off when the loss is determined or within the time frames specified in the classification policy, whichever is shorter.

The classification policy also states that if an institution can clearly document that a past-due loan is well secured and in the process of collection, and collection will occur regardless of delinquency status, the loan need not be classified. The policy describes a well-secured loan as collateralized by a perfected security interest in, or pledges of, real or personal property, including securities with an estimable value, less cost to sell, sufficient to recover the recorded investment in the loan, and a reasonable return on the amount. This category also includes loans well-secured by marketable collateral and in the process of collection, loans for which claims are filed against solvent estates, and loans supported by valid insurance claims. Examiners should note, however, that "in the process of collection" means that either a collection effort or legal action is proceeding and is reasonably expected to result in recovery of the loan balance or its restoration to a current status, generally within the next 90 days.[68]

One special classification case pertains to secured consumer debt discharged in a Chapter 7 bankruptcy proceeding. The classification policy requires secured loans in bankruptcy to be charged down to collateral value, less costs to sell, within 60 days of notification from the bankruptcy court, unless the bank can clearly demonstrate and document that repayment is likely to occur. OCC guidance[69] reiterates that immediate charge-off of amounts exceeding collateral value is not required if an analysis indicates that orderly repayment is likely to occur after the bankruptcy discharge. Any repayment analysis supporting that contention should contain evidence and documentation that the following three factors exist:

- The existence of orderly repayment terms for structured collection of debt without the existence of undue payment shock or need to refinance a balloon amount.
- A history of payment performance demonstrating the borrower's ongoing commitment to satisfy the debt before and through the bankruptcy proceeding.

---

[67] Refer to OCC Bulletin 2014-4, "Secured Consumer Debt Discharged in Chapter 7 Bankruptcy: Supervisory Expectations," for more information on regulatory expectations.

[68] Refer to footnote 54.

[69] Refer to footnote 54.

- The consideration of post-discharge capacity indicating the borrower can make future required payments from recurring, verified income.

Standards for evaluating post-discharge repayment capacity should mirror established ability-to-repay requirements for new loans or sustainable loan modification programs. Banks may use income and debt information from bankruptcy proceedings if such information is available and reliable. Documentation should enable a third party (such as a person responsible for the control function within the bank, an examiner, or an auditor) to reasonably reconstruct the analysis and accept the conclusion after the fact. If the factors considered clearly demonstrate that repayment in full is likely to occur despite the bankruptcy discharge, the loan may remain in accrual status at the existing recorded balance.[70] All loans subject to a bankruptcy proceeding but not fully charged off should be monitored separately and charged down to the fair value of collateral (less costs to sell) if they subsequently become 60 days past due.

These guidelines are designed to help identify troubled borrowers within retail portfolios. Actual credit losses on individual retail credits should be recorded when the institution becomes aware of the loss, but in no case should the charge-off exceed the time frames stated in the classification policy. The policy also does not preclude examiners from classifying individual retail credit loans exhibiting signs of credit weakness regardless of delinquency status. Similarly, an examiner may classify retail portfolios when underwriting standards are weak and present unreasonable credit risk, or when account management practices are deficient.

The key premise of a delinquency-based classification approach is that regular payment performance is a reliable signal of a borrower's ongoing willingness and ability to repay. This is especially true when loans are well structured (e.g., fully amortizing, terms consistent with the use of the proceeds). Less structured payment requirements (e.g., interest-only, negative amortization, extended maturity, or balloon payments) weaken the reliability of payment performance as a proxy for credit quality, because the borrower may be required to obtain some other source of funds to satisfy the debt by maturity (e.g., sale of the asset, cash reserves, or additional financing). As payment performance alone becomes less useful, examiners should expect banks to use other supplemental methods to identify and categorize risk.

Lenders should also be diligent about identifying potential credit problems before delinquency or an obvious credit event (e.g., a bankruptcy or deceased obligor) occurs. This diligence is especially important for products with low minimum monthly payments or principal deferral features (e.g., interest-only or negative amortization), because payment performance may not be a reliable proxy for the true level of risk. Banks with complex or higher-inherent-risk products should supplement delinquency-based monitoring with risk ratings or segmentation systems that differentiate credit risk within the performing segment of the portfolio. Segmentation refers to grouping exposures according to the borrower risk characteristics (e.g., credit score, debt-to-income ratio, and delinquency) and exposure risk

---

[70] Refer to footnote 67.

characteristics (e.g., product type and LTV ratio). Segmentation approaches vary, but tend to follow three broad principles:

- **Meaningful risk differentiation:** Segmentation or ratings systems should stratify risk based on key risk drivers that discriminate among risk levels, allowing management to monitor and evaluate portfolio quality, mix, and migration over time.
- **Reliable characteristics:** Ratings (or segments) should use borrower and exposure risk characteristics that reliably and consistently differentiate the risk among segments.
- **Consistency:** Ratings or segment definitions should be reasonably consistent over time so users become accustomed to criteria and application.

For most retail lending products, banks focus on the borrower's financial condition rather than the asset financed because the primary source of repayment is normally the borrower's personal income or assets. The most common approach uses credit scores as a proxy for risk ratings, and uses segmented credit score bands to differentiate risk within the portfolio. This approach tends to be effective, as long as score bands meaningfully differentiate risk levels and are applied consistently over time. For some products, collateral may be important enough to adjust borrower ratings (e.g., residential real estate), although most adjustments are minor until the credit reaches problem status (i.e., substandard or worse). Ratings or scores should reflect current borrower risk at any point in time, meaning examiners should expect to see ratings or scores assigned at inception and updated periodically as the borrower's financial condition changes.

Understanding portfolio composition at a certain point, and over time, is critical to monitoring credit exposure and adjusting credit strategies. Examiners should expect credit scores and segmentation systems that extend beyond the problem asset classifications (substandard, doubtful, and loss) for large or more complex portfolios. Well-implemented ratings and segmentation systems span the entire portfolio, supporting prudent risk management and the ongoing analysis of concentrations, problem credits, and the adequacy of loan-loss reserves.

Stress Testing to Understand Portfolio Vulnerabilities

Sound credit risk management also involves considering the performance, stability, and quality of retail credit portfolios under a range of economic and market conditions.[71] Bank management can use stress testing to establish and support reasonable risk appetite and tolerance levels, set concentration limits, adjust business strategies, and appropriately plan for and maintain adequate capital levels. Varying, or "stressing," expected results can identify important links among economic downturns, market events, and liquidity conditions that could change portfolio performance in unexpected ways. Factors considered may vary by product, market segment, and the portfolio's size and complexity, but each has the same objective—evaluating risk beyond the expected case, and considering and quantifying the impact of less favorable conditions. These "what if" exercises can be extremely useful for a

---

[71] Refer to footnote 60 for the OCC's expectations for stress testing for all banks.

retail portfolio, revealing undetected areas of exposure in time to consider possible alternatives.

Stress test exercises can range from simple changes in financial or economic variables to the use of sophisticated financial models. Baseline exercises for retail portfolios stress core factors such as delinquency, loss, and recovery rates for their effect on capital, earnings, or liquidity. Advanced approaches consider variables such as attrition or prepayment rates, revolving-product utilization rates, credit score distributions, and secondary market liquidity for loans or asset-backed securities. The retail credit portfolio's size, materiality to bank earnings, and product complexity should dictate the scope of stress tests. Inputs should be reliable and relate directly to the subject portfolio (e.g., the loss history is specific to the product evaluated, not a blend of several or all products), and assumptions should be reasonable. For large retail portfolios, stress testing and scenario analysis should occur at least annually for each major product line and more frequently for products with significant revenue implications or a higher risk profile.

Regardless of the method used, the process should be clearly documented, rational, and easily understood by the bank's board and senior management. Senior management should review test outcomes and take appropriate action when results are not within agreed upon tolerances. Contingency plans should be considered for certain scenarios, including hedging against outcomes or reducing exposure levels. The board and senior management should use this information to determine whether policy, limit, or other changes, such as updating exposure parameters within the risk appetite, are warranted.

Allowance for Loan and Lease Losses

The allowance for loan and lease losses (ALLL) is one of the most significant estimates in the bank's financial statements, and establishing a sound and consistent process is a primary responsibility for the board and senior management. This responsibility also includes maintaining policies and procedures, model estimates, internal controls, and qualitative adjustments that are consistent with generally accepted accounting principles (GAAP) and support an appropriate ALLL.[72]

Examiners should refer to OCC Bulletin 2006-47, "Allowance for Loan and Lease Losses (ALLL): Guidance and Frequently Asked Questions (FAQs) on the ALLL"; OCC Bulletin 2012-6, "Interagency Guidance on ALLL Estimation Practices for Junior Liens: Guidance on Junior Liens"; and the "Allowance for Loan and Lease Losses" booklet of the *Comptroller's*

---

[72] The Financial Accounting Standards Board issued a new expected credit loss standard, Accounting Standards Update (ASU) No. 2016-13, Topic 326, "Financial Instruments–Credit Losses," commonly referred to as the current expected credit losses model, in June 2016. The standard is effective for U.S. Securities and Exchange Commission filers in fiscal years and interim periods beginning after December 15, 2019. For public business entities that are not Securities and Exchange Commission filers, the standard takes effect in fiscal years and interim periods beginning after December 15, 2020. For private companies, it takes effect in fiscal years beginning after December 15, 2020. Until the new standard becomes effective, institutions should follow current GAAP along with the related supervisory guidance on the ALLL. Visit the OCC's website at www.occ.gov for additional information regarding the current expected credit loss model.

Handbook for the applicable accounting standards and other considerations for the ALLL. For retail credit, the analysis includes determining whether the bank's practices

- conform to the uniform retail classification guidance.
- recognize charge-offs in a timely manner and accurately.
- identify, segment, and track performance of higher-risk product segments in a prudent manner.
- include sound governance, controls, and maintenance over models used to estimate or provide data to estimate the ALLL.
- provide reasonable and reconcilable support for qualitative factors used to account for environmental differences between quantitative estimates and current market and economic conditions.

The ALLL analysis is more reliable when the bank's portfolios are appropriately segmented into groups of loans with similar risk characteristics. Homogeneous pools generally start at the product level, although most large or complex portfolios are further segmented. For example, high-LTV (over 100 percent) HELOCs, or an unsecured credit card offered to subprime borrowers, may exhibit substantially higher losses than the general product averages; while automobile loans originated through a specific dealer or group of dealers may perform significantly better.

Internal Controls and Control Functions

Internal controls are the policies, operating procedures, and adherence reviews providing assurance that adherence to policies and prudent risk mitigation actions occur. Effective control systems help managers measure performance, make decisions, evaluate processes, and limit risks. Control system reviews can detect mistakes caused by carelessness, errors in judgment, or unclear instructions, in addition to fraud or deliberate noncompliance with laws, regulations, and bank policies. The laws and regulations that establish minimum requirements for internal controls are 12 CFR 30, appendix A, "Interagency Guidelines Establishing Standards for Safety and Soundness"; 12 CFR 363, "Annual Independent Audits and Reporting Requirements";[73] and 15 USC 78m, "Securities and Exchange Act of 1934, Periodical and Other Reports."[74]

The bank's board and senior management are responsible for promoting a sound control environment. Ongoing monitoring should be part of normal operations for each retail credit area. Business unit staff is responsible for implementing effective internal controls and should self-assess its processes regularly. For large or complex portfolios, a quality assurance function should regularly assess whether processes are achieving desired results, and an

---

[73] 12 CFR 363, "Annual Independent Audits and Reporting Requirements," applies to any insured depository institution with respect to any fiscal year in which its consolidated total assets as of the beginning of such fiscal year are $500 million or more. This regulation establishes minimum requirements for audit committee membership and the need for independent reviews of financial statements for these banks.

[74] 15 USC 78m requires banks and holding companies with a class of securities registered pursuant to the Securities Exchange Act of 1934 to develop and maintain a system of internal accounting controls.

---

independent quality control function should periodically evaluate whether loans and loan documentation conform to established criteria. Internal and external audit also have key responsibilities and should independently assess control system effectiveness.

There are many types of control activities, including preventive, detective, and corrective controls. Some common credit-related controls within a retail lending business include the following:

- **Compliance measures:** To ensure that the bank and its personnel comply with applicable laws and regulations, as well as internal policies and procedures.
- **Information integrity:** To ensure that financial performance and credit risk information included in the bank's internal management reports, financial statements, and supervisory reports are prepared in accordance with the applicable accounting framework and relevant supervisory guidance.
- **Risk assessment and risk identification processes:** To ensure that credit exposures are monitored objectively, accurately, and consistently. An effective risk assessment is most often done through well-defined, independent processes, including
  - a borrower grading or segmentation system that is consistently applied, accurately rates important credit risk characteristics, identifies changes in credit quality in a timely manner, and prompts appropriate actions or responses.
  - credit assessment at the individual borrower level and broader portfolio levels by grouping exposures based on identified shared credit risk characteristics.
  - effective model risk governance[75] that ensures that models employ and generate accurate, consistent, and predictive estimates on an ongoing basis. This governance includes establishing policies and procedures setting out the accountability and reporting structure of the model validation process, internal standards for assessing and approving changes to the models, and reporting of the outcome of model validation.
  - clear formal communication and coordination among the bank's credit risk staff, financial reporting staff, senior management, the board, and others who are involved in the credit risk assessment and measurement process, as applicable (e.g., evidenced by written policies and procedures, management reports, and committee minutes).
  - an internal loan review or credit audit function that independently evaluates the effectiveness of the bank's credit assessment and measurement systems and processes, including the credit risk grading system.

Tests for each control activity should be systematic and include reporting and escalation processes for when issues arise. Effective discipline is important. When noncompliance is found, timely and effective corrective action should follow. If actions are not appropriate, the risk governance process loses credibility.

Examiners should determine whether controls are commensurate with the environment and markets in which the bank operates, as well as with the bank's size, complexity, and risk profile. Large, complex banks with diverse lending activities may face more difficult control

---

[75] Refer to OCC Bulletin 2011-12, "Sound Practices for Model Risk Management: Supervisory Guidance on Model Risk Management."

issues than community banks with less varied activities, and the nature of internal controls should reflect those differences.

Credit risk control functions help maintain credit risk exposure within parameters set by the board and senior management. Active control functions are important given the wide range of staff that typically can create credit exposure for the bank. Establishing and enforcing internal controls, operating limits, and other practices help maintain credit risk exposures within acceptable levels, and these systems collectively provide assurance that account officers and others are working in accordance with specified policies and operating procedures.

For a retail credit portfolio, control functions typically include risk management, loan review, third-party relationship risk management, model risk management, quality assurance, compliance review, and internal audit. Examiners should expect the form and scope of control functions to vary based on the bank's size, products, risk profile, and target markets. Most importantly, control functions should operate as independent, objective methods to evaluate the efficacy of internal controls, the adequacy of operational and reporting processes, and the level of risk in the products or portfolios. Independent reviews by these groups help the board and senior management evaluate credit approval, credit administration, and portfolio management practices; determine the accuracy of internal risk identification systems; and judge whether the business is properly monitoring risk from all likely sources. New products and emerging technologies should receive special attention given their potential to change the bank's risk profile if poorly conceived or implemented. Control function involvement during new product planning helps with the proper assessment of operating procedures, risk identification, and testing before implementation.

One guiding principle for these independent control functions is the concept of an "effective challenge" of processes, activities, and controls. Effective challenge refers to critical analysis by objective, competent parties who can identify risk management limitations and assumptions and influence appropriate changes. The existence of an effective challenge depends on a combination of objectiveness, competence, and influence. Challenges are more likely to be viewed as objective, and therefore accepted by all relevant parties (e.g., business lines, the board, senior management, other control functions, and bank regulators), when the party providing the challenge is independent from the credit approval and credit administration processes, and has control over the scope, timing, and depth of their reviews. Competence is important since technical knowledge and risk evaluation skills are necessary to conduct credible analysis and suggest appropriate enhancements. Finally, challenges are unlikely to be effective without the ability to influence appropriate actions to address credit issues and deficient practices. Such influence comes from a combination of explicit authority, stature within the organization, and commitment and support from higher levels of management, as well as the board.

The control functions discussed in this section build on one another to support efficient and effective oversight. Examiners should consider deficiencies within each function separately, as well as how issues may affect the risk management framework overall.

Risk Management Function

Risk management generally refers to the process of identifying, measuring, monitoring, and controlling risk. Risk management can also describe a department or function within the bank responsible for ensuring that lending activities and program initiatives stay within risk tolerances and operating guidelines established by the board and senior management.

The risk management function is mainly responsible for the early and accurate identification of existing and potential problems. This function identifies and monitors risk levels through ongoing evaluations of underwriting, marketing, account management, and portfolio management activities. Risk management's role is especially important when market conditions, products, or the bank's strategy changes, since these changes often raise risk levels before delinquency and charge-off signals appear. For retail lending, a risk management function is typically responsible for

- determining whether appropriate credit standards and practices are established and implemented.
- determining whether exceptions to established policies and operating procedures are promptly identified, approved, reported, and evaluated.
- determining whether credit scoring and other models are effectively developed, deployed, and maintained.
- determining whether account management, collections, and workout activities are prudent and appropriate.
- analyzing the impact of underwriting and account management practices and strategies.
- monitoring portfolio quality and analyzing performance.
- reporting findings and suggested remedial actions to senior management and the board.

The risk management function may be centralized or decentralized, depending on the bank's size and the complexity of retail lending activities. For example, in many community banks, an employee may have risk management responsibilities in addition to his or her primary role as loan officer, auditor, or cashier, and some functions, such as loan review or internal audit, may be outsourced to third parties. The largest banks have dedicated risk management units for each major business line, and often have a corporate risk management group for consumer lending overall. Community banks are not required to hire a full-time risk officer. Examiners should expect, however, that even for community banks with large or complex retail portfolios, a member of senior management, preferably outside of the credit risk-taking function, to have responsibility for monitoring and opining on the risk profile and retail credit risk management practices of the bank. However executed, effective risk management requires reliable, objective, and thorough analyses of the standards and practices influencing loan portfolio quality and performance. The board and senior management are responsible for ensuring that the necessary risk management tasks are performed, and that those performing these tasks have the appropriate level of expertise, independence, and management support to be effective.

Heightened Standards

Independent risk management should oversee the covered bank's risk-taking activities and assess risks and issues independent of frontline units. In fulfilling these responsibilities, independent risk management should, among other things

- take primary responsibility and be held accountable by the CEO and the board of directors for designing a comprehensive written risk governance framework that is commensurate with the size, complexity, and risk profile of the covered bank.
- identify and assess, on an ongoing basis, the covered bank's material aggregate risks, and use such assessments to determine if actions need to be taken to strengthen risk management or reduce risk, given changes in the covered bank's risk profile or other conditions.
- establish and adhere to enterprise policies that include concentration risk limits. Such policies should state how aggregate risks are effectively identified, measured, monitored, and controlled, consistent with the covered bank's established risk appetite and all policies and processes established within the risk governance framework.
- identify and communicate material risks and significant instances when independent risk management's assessment of risk differs from that of a frontline unit, or when a frontline unit is not adhering to the risk governance framework.
- identify and communicate material risks and significant instances when independent risk management's assessment of risk differs from the CEO's assessment, or when the CEO is not adhering to, or holding frontline units accountable for adhering to, the risk governance framework.[76]

Loan Review

The purpose of the loan review function[77] is to provide regular independent assessments of credit risk, helping the board and senior management understand and monitor portfolio quality. Assessments should consider credit risk practices and exposures in the context of the established risk appetite, policies and operating procedures, business strategies, and industry and peer performance. Assessments should address the adequacy of lending policies and compliance with applicable laws and regulations, as well as consistency with supervisory guidance.

Each bank should have a written loan review policy reviewed and approved by the board at least annually. The policy should address

- qualifications and independence of loan review personnel.
- frequency, scope, and depth of reviews.
- review of findings and follow-up.
- work paper and report distribution.

---

[76] For more information, refer to 12 CFR 30, appendix D, II.C.2, "Role and Responsibilities of Independent Risk Management."

[77] Loan review (also referred to as credit review) is a key internal control and an element of the safety and soundness standards described in the "Interagency Guidelines for Establishing Standards for Safety and Soundness" found in appendix A of 12 CFR 30, "Safety and Soundness Standards." For more information, refer to the "Loan Portfolio Management" booklet of the *Comptroller's Handbook* and attachment 1 of the "Interagency Policy Statement on the Allowance for Loan and Lease Losses," conveyed in OCC Bulletin 2006-47, "Allowance for Loan and Lease Losses (ALLL): Guidance and Frequently Asked Questions (FAQs) on the ALLL."

Loan review staff should have a strong, fundamental understanding of both sound retail lending practices and the internal lending guidelines for each bank product. Loan review should be independent of the credit approval process, with no primary responsibilities for loan approval, administration, collections, or customer service. In large banks, this need for independence generally requires a separate department staffed with specialists whose only responsibilities are loan review. A completely separate loan review function may not be cost-effective for community banks, but some level of independence is necessary.

Loan review's scope should include an assessment of risk in each major retail product or significant product segment at least annually, or more frequently when internal or external factors indicate potential issues. Retail reviews should focus on judgmental and automated underwriting; controls and prudent use of credit scoring, risk-based pricing, and account management initiatives; and collections, workout, and portfolio management activities.

For retail portfolios, risk assessments should address compliance with

- internal credit policies and operating procedures.
- loan classification and segmentation practices.
- internal controls and business rules pertaining to models or other automated decision tools.
- laws and regulations, including those relevant to consumer protection, BSA, anti-money laundering (AML), and U.S. sanctions obligations administered by the Office of Foreign Assets Control. Risk assessments should also address consistency with regulatory guidance.

Reviews by the loan review function should generally include representative loan samples to determine whether policies and operating procedures are followed in practice. Samples should provide reasonable assurance that results have identified potential issues with risk identification and credit quality deterioration. Retail loan samples typically include

- new loans since the last review.
- performing loans from each targeted product.
- past-due, nonaccrual, renewed, and restructured loans.
- loans approved as exceptions to policy.
- loans in temporary or permanent workout programs.
- loans that are part of identified concentrations of credit risk.

All reviews should confirm specific aspects of the loans selected, including

- credit quality, including underwriting and borrower performance.
- sufficiency of credit and collateral documentation.
- proper lien perfection for secured loans.
- proper approvals.
- compliance with internal policies and procedures (such as re-aging and nonaccrual) and applicable laws and regulations.

- appropriate identification and measurement of individually impaired loans, and timeliness of charge-offs.
- appropriate and timely identification of problem loans and problem loan segments.

Monitoring systems should track the status of recommendations and corrective action by business line management. Loan review should maintain a schedule of open and resolved issues, and hold management accountable for timely resolution. Regular reporting by loan review to senior management and the board should include topics such as noted deficiencies and identified weaknesses remaining unresolved beyond scheduled periods, reviews that result in less than satisfactory ratings, emerging risk themes, and the scope of future loan review coverage.

Third-Party Relationship Risk Management

A third-party service provider is any entity that performs a function or provides a service on the bank's behalf, by contract or otherwise. Third-party service providers can include affiliates, brokers, dealers, data processors, consultants, attorneys, collection companies, marketing firms and telemarketers, and modeling firms. Retail lenders often outsource components of their credit operations to third parties, most often for access to expertise, technology, acquisition channels, and cost savings.

Reliance on third parties introduces risk exposure that must be managed. This need for risk management is particularly true for retail businesses when third parties often have significant customer contact or handle compliance with laws or regulations and help to establish consistency with regulatory guidance. This type of reliance on third parties increases the importance of a sound third-party relationship risk management program.[78]

A bank should adopt a risk management process commensurate with the level of risk and complexity of its third-party relationships. A third-party risk management program's primary objectives are to determine whether the service provider's actions are consistent with the bank's expectations and operating standards; that the third-party service provider meets all relevant legal and contractual requirements; and that the third party has the financial capacity to deliver the contracted services in the specified manner. Third-party relationships often involve the use of subcontractors to provide some or all of the services. When this occurs, examiners should consider whether the bank's oversight program adequately evaluates the volume and types of subcontracted activities, as well as the third party's ability to assess, monitor, and mitigate risks from its use of subcontractors. Examiners should also expect more comprehensive oversight when services involve critical activities (e.g., telemarketing, collections, and foreclosure services) or critical shared services (e.g., information technology). Risk management of third parties providing critical activities or shared services should be commensurate with the critical nature of the relationship.

---

[78] For further guidance, refer to OCC Bulletin 2013-29, "Third-Party Relationships: Risk Management Guidance."

Model Risk Management

Retail credit management often involves models and assumption-based estimates for loan originations (including automated underwriting systems), account management, collections, and portfolio management. The nature of retail credit portfolios—i.e., many accounts, relatively small balances, technology-intensive operations, and numerous transactions (including defaults)—lends itself well to a modeling environment. Retail credit models commonly include credit scoring, behavior scoring, collections, stress testing, and capital and ALLL estimates. Well-managed model use can significantly improve business decisions and enhance profitability. There are associated costs, however, beginning with devoting the resources necessary to properly develop, implement, and validate models. Indirect costs also include the possible adverse consequences of poor decisions based on models that are unreliable or misused.

Model risk tends to increase with model complexity, broader use, and the uncertainty or unreliability of inputs or assumptions. Model risk is also affected by interaction and dependencies among models; reliance on common assumptions, data, or methodologies; and the potential for other factors that could adversely affect several models and their outputs at the same time. Examiners should expect management to actively identify potential sources of model risk and take appropriate steps to mitigate exposures.[79] These steps should include an effective oversight framework with clear authority and responsibility to restrict model use when necessary.

Even skilled modeling development practices and robust validation do not eliminate model risk for retail credit businesses. Other tools are necessary, including established business limits on model use, monitoring of model performance, adjusting or revising models over time, and supplementing model results with other analysis and information. In banks with complex or large retail portfolios (in actual size or in relation to capital), models and model output tend to have a material impact on business decisions related to credit, risk management, and capital and liquidity planning. The model risk management framework for those banks should be extensive and rigorous enough to address the level and magnitude of potential risks.

Quality Control and Quality Assurance

Control responsibilities exist both inside and outside of the business line. Within the business line, a combination of quality control and quality assurance reviews ensures operational compliance and considers whether established processes are appropriate. Both quality control and quality assurance checks are important, and examiners should determine whether each is an effective part of normal business processes.

Quality control is concerned with adherence to expectations. Quality control reviews confirm that bank personnel are adhering to established policies and operating procedures. Examples

---

[79] OCC Bulletins 1997-24, "Credit Scoring Models: Examination Guidance," and 2011-12, "Sound Practices for Model Risk Management: Supervisory Guidance on Model Risk Management," provide additional guidance for model development, implementation, and validation.

of quality control activities include document reviews, model governance reviews, underwriting tests, and reviews over the use of modifications, rewrites, and renewals.

Quality assurance focuses on whether the processes are appropriate and deliver the desired results. Examples of quality assurance tests include process checklists, project audits, decision trees, and process and standards development.

Management at most large banks, or banks with higher risk profiles, recognize the importance of objective, independent quality control and quality assurance functions and establish units independent of the business lines. In small banks, each function may exist within the business line through a rotation of duties or other process that promotes a level of independent review. Whether housed within the business line or as part of a fully independent control function, both quality control and quality assurance functions should be outside of the direct supervision of the staff performing the processes under review. This independence is necessary to promote credible and reliable results. It is also important that audit or another independent control function routinely review and validate the processes, results, and follow-up actions in response to the reviews.

Compliance Review

Compliance with laws and regulations, including those relevant to consumer protection, BSA, anti-money laundering (AML), and U.S. sanctions obligations administered by the Office of Foreign Assets Control, should be a high priority for a retail credit business. The risks of noncompliance are significant in terms of financial exposure and damage to the bank's reputation. Therefore, ensuring that processes address compliance with relevant laws and regulations and consistency with regulatory guidance warrants management's ongoing attention and diligence.

An effective compliance management program is an important control function. The compliance function is a group that determines whether the processes to promote compliance are working as intended. In large operations, the compliance function reviews quality assurance results and performs targeted process reviews (e.g., review payment processing for compliance with applicable laws). The bank's BSA/AML compliance program should be structured to adequately address the bank's BSA risk profile, as identified by its risk assessment. Compliance also monitors consumer complaints to identify issues or concerns resulting from policy weaknesses, the failure to comply with bank policies and procedures, or potential violations of laws and regulations. In community banks, the compliance officer generally has a process for regularly testing application and loan samples and most likely is responsible for monitoring and responding to consumer complaints, or compliance review may be outsourced to an independent third party.

Regardless of bank size, the compliance function should be sufficiently staffed and well trained and independent of the operating units. Results of compliance reviews should be reported directly to the board and senior management.

Internal Audit

Internal audit objectively and independently reviews and evaluates retail credit activities, including accounting systems, management reporting, and operations. Internal audit provides the board with important information regarding the efficiency and effectiveness of credit risk management activities, specifically, whether existing internal controls are sufficient and working as intended. Internal audit does this by

- evaluating the reliability, adequacy, and effectiveness of accounting, operating, and administrative controls.
- determining whether internal controls result in prompt and accurate recording of transactions and safeguarding of assets.
- determining whether the bank complies with laws and regulations and adheres to established bank policies.
- determining whether management is taking appropriate steps to address current and prior control deficiencies and audit report recommendations.

Retail audit reviews tend to be process oriented with a heavy emphasis on internal control questionnaires and operating procedures governing the loan application, documentation, loan closing, and collection processes. Operational and compliance reviews often focus on the forms related to disclosures, applications, and promissory notes, as well as other forms used in the various lending transactions. Most audit reviews include credit and loan documentation file samples to review specific transactions for compliance once policies and operating procedures are considered adequate. Many internal audit reviews also include denied loan applications and notifications to ensure proper notices were sent to applicants, as well as the proper processing of cash disbursements, loan payoffs, and loan charge-offs. For banks with large or complex retail portfolios, internal audit should also review and reconcile important management reports, including the accuracy and timeliness of reports provided to the board and senior management. It is important that auditors systematically cycle through all retail lending products within scheduled and defined time frames to promote regular and thorough coverage of all retail activities.

Internal audit should be independent and report directly to the board (or an audit committee of the board).[80] In most cases, internal audit is responsible for reviewing the adequacy of the other control function processes, such as loan review, in addition to its own operational reviews. As part of its reviews, internal audit should communicate effectively to understand the scope and findings of reviews completed by other control functions and the responsiveness of management to open issues. This close contact can help internal audit understand how to leverage other control system reviews and use resources most efficiently.

---

[80] For more information on the OCC's expectations for effective audit functions, refer to the "Internal and External Audits" booklet of the *Comptroller's Handbook*.

Heightened Standards

Internal audit should, among other things, determine whether the covered bank's risk governance framework complies with the applicable regulatory standards and is appropriate for the bank's size, complexity, and risk profile. Internal audit should maintain a complete and current inventory of all the covered bank's material processes, product lines, services, and functions, and assess the risks, including emerging risks, associated with each, which collectively provide a basis for the audit plan.[81]

---

[81] For more information, refer to 12 CFR 30, appendix D, II.C.3, "Role and Responsibilities of Internal Audit."

Examination Procedures

This booklet contains expanded procedures for examining specialized activities or specific products or services that warrant extra attention beyond the core assessment contained in the "Community Bank Supervision," "Large Bank Supervision," and "Federal Branches and Agencies Supervision" booklets of the *Comptroller's Handbook*. Examiners determine which expanded procedures to use, if any, during examination planning or after drawing preliminary conclusions during the core assessment.

Scope

These procedures are designed to help examiners tailor the examination to each bank and determine the scope of the retail lending examination. This determination should consider work performed by internal and external auditors and other independent risk control functions and by other examiners on related areas. Examiners need to perform only those objectives and steps that are relevant to the scope of the examination as determined by the following objective. Seldom will every objective or step of the procedures be necessary.

Objective: To determine the scope of the examination of retail lending and identify examination objectives and activities necessary to meet the needs of the supervisory strategy for the bank.

1. Review the following sources of information and note any previously identified issues related to retail credit risk management requiring follow-up:

   - Supervisory strategy
   - Examiner-in-charge's scope memorandum
   - The OCC's information system and OCC reports
   - Previous reports of examination and work papers
   - Internal and external audit reports and work papers
   - Bank management's responses to previous reports of examination and audit reports
   - Customer complaints and litigation
   - Results of reports such as the Uniform Bank Performance Reports and Canary

2. Obtain results from the Uniform Bank Performance Report, and other OCC reports or analytical tools relating to retail lending. Identify trends and changes in growth rates, portfolio composition, concentrations, portfolio performance, pricing, and other factors that may affect the bank's risk profile.

3. Obtain and review policies, procedures, and reports that bank management uses to supervise retail lending and retail credit risk management, including internal risk assessments.

4. Obtain and review the minutes from the oversight and risk committees related to retail credit since the last full scope or target examination.

5. Obtain and review the organizational chart for retail credit, including its key executives and risk managers, as well as a description of the retail risk management framework.

6. Determine if there were any significant changes in the structure or approach to retail lending or credit risk management since the last examination. For example, identify changes in credit policies, key personnel, portfolio strategies, risk tolerances, concentration or risk limits, control systems, third-party relationships, credit-related models, delivery channels, loan volumes, or target markets.

7. Determine whether any litigation, either filed or expected, is associated with the bank's retail credit activities. For existing or pending litigation, determine expected costs or other implications (e.g., reputation risk).

8. Based on an analysis of information obtained in the previous steps and input from the examiner-in-charge, determine the scope and objectives for the retail credit risk management examination.

9. Select from the following examination procedures the steps necessary to meet examination objectives and the supervisory strategy.

Quantity of Risk

Conclusion: The quantity of each associated risk is (low, moderate, or high).

Objective: Determine the quantity of risk associated with retail credit activities.

1. Evaluate changes to the size, composition, growth rate, and performance of the retail portfolio since the last examination. Consider

   - changes in products, product mix, marketing channels, underwriting standards, operations, or technology.
   - rapid growth in accounts, segments, or products. Consider dollars outstanding and unfunded commitments.
   - changes in the composition or mix of performing loans (credit score distribution, geographic mix, products, loan structures, etc.).
   - changes in the level or type of problem, classified, past-due, or nonperforming assets.
   - changes in charge-off volumes overall or within products, segments, or portfolios (dollars, percentages, or number of accounts).
   - changes in workout or modification program volumes (temporary or permanent) overall, or within products, segments, or portfolios.
   - significant concentrations (industry, geographic, product, or borrower segments).
   - introduction of new or significantly revised products.
   - levels, trends, and performance of loans made as exceptions to loan policies.
   - levels, trends, and performance of accounts that have been re-aged, extended, deferred, renewed, or rewritten.
   - dependence on third parties for originations, account management, or collection activities.

2. Review the strategic and business plans for retail lending overall and for each major product.[82] Evaluate how plan implementation may affect the quantity of credit risk. Consider

   - growth objectives and potential sources of new loans.
   - changes in target markets or geographic footprints.
   - emphasis on high-risk products, loan structures, or customers.
   - permissible products and loan structures.
   - acceptable collateral types or LTV ratio requirements.
   - new or growing concentrations of credit.

---

[82] While conducting reviews of lending activities, examiners should be alert to, and discuss with the examiner-in-charge, policies, practices, or product terms that could indicate discriminatory, unfair, deceptive, abusive, or predatory lending issues.

3. Analyze the level, composition, and trends of underwriting and loan documentation exceptions, and determine the potential impact on the quantity of risk. Consider trends of exceptions to

- underwriting or credit approval standards.
- loan documentation standards.
- account management, collections, and use of workout programs.
- concentration or risk limits.

4. Evaluate management's success with projecting portfolio size, composition, and performance by comparing the current year's results with planned or projected performance in the previous business plans. Review the retail portfolio as a whole and any significant product or product segments.

5. Assess the level of inherent risk in loan structures, target markets, and credit underwriting. Consider the relative volumes (percentage of accounts or loan balances) of outstanding loans for

- loan structures, considering four main categories:
  - fixed-rate, fully amortizing loans.
  - loans that amortize, but not completely over the loan term (i.e., balloons).
  - loans that permit interest-only monthly payments.
  - loans that permit monthly payments that can be less than interest and fees (i.e., negative amortization).
- target borrowers, considering three main segments:
  - prime, or high-quality, low-default borrowers. These typically receive the bank's (and market's) best loan pricing and terms.
  - near-prime. These borrowers have some characteristics of prime but also have evidence of increased risk. Examples include unverifiable income, credit problems recently resolved, or problems requiring a waiver or exception to the bank's current underwriting criteria. These borrowers generally receive loan pricing higher than prime customers.
  - subprime. These can include thin credit files, high existing debt levels, poor payment histories, or other credit quality issues. These borrowers tend to pay the highest interest rates in the market.
- level of credit underwriting due diligence, in five main categories:
  - income and employment verifications.
  - total monthly debt service consideration.
  - total debt level consideration in relation to income or assets.
  - consideration of ability to repay fully drawn lines for all existing and proposed open-end credit.
  - consideration of potential interest rate increases for variable rate debt.

6. Assess the impact of the bank's securitization, loan purchase and sale programs, credit derivatives, or other liquidity or concentration management tools on the quantity of risk. Consider the

- relative significance to portfolio composition and risk.
- quality of loans in the programs.
- potential impact of any required loan repurchases.
- volume of credit derivatives or other products.
- impact on revenues and portfolio profitability.

7. Analyze the volume, trend, and significance of litigation and consumer complaints related to retail credit products. Discuss significant litigation and complaints with bank management. Determine the risk to capital and impact on reputation risk. Also determine the appropriateness of corrective action and follow-up processes.

8. Evaluate the results of any stress testing of the retail portfolio (or significant products). Consider the sensitivity of portfolios (or significant portfolio segments) to interest rate changes, collateral value declines, or profitability due to likely or near-term stressed conditions.

9. Assess the retail portfolio's exposure to pending legislative, regulatory, or accounting changes that may materially affect the portfolio.

Quality of Risk Management

Conclusion: The quality of risk management is (strong, satisfactory, insufficient, or weak).

The conclusion on risk management considers the following risks associated with retail credit risk management.

Retail Credit Risk Governance

Risk management concerns the identification, analysis, assessment, control, and mitigation of unacceptable risks. The retail credit governance program describes the framework under which the bank manages its exposure to retail credit risk.

Objective: Determine whether the board has established an organizational structure responsible for monitoring retail credit risk across the bank that is commensurate with the size, complexity, and risk profile of the portfolio.

1. Determine whether the retail credit risk governance program is explicit, well documented, and well communicated. Consider whether the program has been

   - documented in writing.
   - designed by qualified individuals.
   - supported by clear delegations of authority and responsibility for risk management activities.
   - subject to annual review by the board or its appropriate committee.
   - applied across the full range of retail lending products and services offered, including significant third-party service providers.

2. Evaluate the structure's depth and consistency given the size, complexity, and risk profile of existing and expected retail lending products. Consider whether the structure clearly establishes

   - oversight responsibilities of the board and management-level committees.
   - policies, operating procedures, and process maps for all significant activities.
   - concentration and risk limits at the business, product, and significant portfolio levels.
   - processes for identifying, approving, monitoring, and analyzing exceptions to policies and operating procedures.
   - standards for effective monitoring reports for all significant activities.
   - systematic adherence checks that assess whether practices conform with established policies and operating procedures.

3. Determine whether a board-level committee has direct oversight of retail credit risk. Consider whether the committee

- has members with appropriate retail credit knowledge and experience.
- has complete access to senior management, credit risk management, and loan review to ask questions or raise issues.
- has explicit authority to obtain advice and assistance from legal, accounting, or other technical areas.
- reviews business plans for each major retail product or business line.
- approves all significant retail credit risk policies.
- regularly reviews reports that monitor adherence to policies, operating procedures, and established risk appetite.
- is consulted promptly on material policy exceptions.
- has a role in developing compensation programs to ensure incentives are consistent with the desired culture.
- has the ability to request ad hoc reports for specific issues or concerns.

4. Document and assess the full spectrum of committees, councils, forums, and working groups within the retail business that identify, assess, or manage credit risk. Obtain and review

- an organizational chart that shows each committee's place in the organization.
- charters and membership for each group.
- the sphere of influence and source of authority for each committee or working group. Consider
  - whether authority is delegated formally or informally to each group.
  - which committees are decision-making vs. informational in nature.
  - how decisions, recommendations, or follow-up tasks flow back to the affected business units.

5. Choose one or more oversight or management committees and obtain and review the group charter, membership, and recent meeting packages. Evaluate whether they provide meaningful input and guidance for their specific areas. Consider whether

- the committee has a clear charter defining required membership, frequency of meetings and reports, documentation of minutes, responsibilities, and accountabilities.
- meeting minutes and discussion recaps indicate that the committee actively and properly assesses risks in its areas.
- meeting materials support the committee's stated objectives.
- the committee plays an active role in reviewing significant changes to credit policies, and reviews policy exception reporting and analyses.
- the committee requests or reviews special reports on an ad hoc or request basis.

6. Choose the retail credit group overall, or select one or more products or business lines that have established risk appetite statements, and determine whether defined standards and procedures exist for how

- risk appetite statements are developed and monitored.
- risk assessment exercises are performed.
- concentration and risk limits consistent with the risk appetite are established.
- business operating plans clearly link to risk appetite statements.
- product-level policies and operating procedures are created, maintained, and amended.
- policy and operating procedure exceptions are identified, monitored, and analyzed.
- loan portfolio quality is monitored and assessed.

7. Obtain risk appetite statements for retail lending overall, and for any individual products or business lines. Determine whether

- a clear link exists between the stated risk appetite and the products or markets the bank pursues.
- risk appetite statements are actionable, with metrics addressing tolerances for important criteria.
- risk limits are quantifiable and measurable, with control parameters (e.g., guidelines and triggers) established relative to significant measures such as portfolio size, mix, growth, profitability, or capital.
- a reassessment of the bank's risk appetite is conducted at least annually, when new business opportunities arise, or when there are changes in risk capacity, operating environment, or other economic factors.

8. Determine how retail credit activities are assessed for compliance with risk appetite statements. Consider whether

- risks can be identified and aggregated within and across legal entities, business lines, products and services, and geographies when measuring against risk tolerances.
- a process exists to identify business units that are operating outside risk appetite parameters, or that are not within the spirit of the risk appetite.
- management has established action plan requirements for when control parameters are breached.
- periodic assessments are presented to the board (or designated committee) on observed risk levels compared with established risk appetite.

Policies

Policies are statements of actions adopted by the bank to pursue certain objectives. Policies guide decisions, often set standards (on risk limits, for example), and should be consistent with the bank's underlying mission, risk appetite, and core values. Policies should be reviewed periodically for effectiveness and approved by the board of directors or designated board committee.

Objective: Determine whether lending policies are consistent with the established risk appetite and comprehensively define risk tolerance, responsibilities, accountabilities, and relevant regulatory requirements.

1. Determine whether established standards define the content and administration of retail credit policies. Consider whether policy administration

    *   requires policies to be reviewed annually by senior management for compatibility with current risk appetites, market conditions, laws, and regulations, and for consistency with regulatory guidance.
    *   specifies board review and approval at inception, during major changes, and at least annually thereafter.
    *   requires policies to link directly to operating procedures and process maps that describe how each policy is implemented.
    *   includes training to help users understand and apply policies, procedures, and process maps.
    *   requires up-to-date chronology logs to record the date and nature of changes.
    *   requires standards to address compliance with applicable laws, rulings, regulations, and accounting guidelines, and consistency with regulatory guidance.
    *   requires periodic review of administration and implementation by independent control functions such as internal audit, external audit, or loan review.

2. Assess whether credit policies establish appropriate criteria and limits for each retail product. Consider whether policies establish

    *   permissible types of loans.
    *   markets and geographic areas in which the bank will lend.
    *   portfolio distribution limits by product, type, and market.
    *   concentration limits (e.g., product, geography, brokers, dealers, and score bands).
    *   guidelines for handling exceptions to established policies and operating procedures.
    *   loan administration procedures, including documentation, disbursement, collateral inspection, collection, and loan review.
    *   loan portfolio monitoring requirements, including timely and adequate reports to the board (or other oversight committee) and senior management.

3. Assess whether credit policies specify loan terms and conditions for each retail product. Consider whether guidelines establish

    *   maximum loan amounts by product and loan type.
    *   maximum loan maturities by product and loan type.
    *   amortization schedules, and standards for the acceptability of nonamortizing loans.
    *   pricing structures.
    *   minimum down payment requirements.
    *   acceptable collateral (e.g., furniture, service contracts, and automobiles) and lien perfection requirements.

- collateral advance rates and LTV limits (if applicable).
- collateral valuation guidelines and methodologies.
- standards for evaluating a borrower's financial capacity and ability to repay.
- standards for evaluating a borrower's willingness to repay.[83]
- guidelines for purchasing loans from correspondents and other third parties.

4. Review the bank's loan and charge-off policies for consistency with the Uniform Retail Credit Classification and Account Management Policy.[84] Consider whether

- retail lending and charge-off policies are consistent with regulatory guidance.
- periodic independent internal control reviews of consistency with the policy occur.
- issues identified during control-system reviews are resolved in an appropriate and effective manner.

5. Determine whether policies for originate-to-sell programs[85] address

- industry and partner selection.
- credit criteria and underwriting standards.
- operational controls for stale inventory, pipeline production, concentrations, and hedging.
- loan repurchase exposures and reserves.
- required monitoring reports and control function reviews.

6. Assess whether policies governing internal controls provide for

- clear lines of authority and responsibility for the adequacy of, and adherence to, established policies.
- effective and systematic risk assessment.
- timely and accurate financial, operational, and regulatory reports.
- adequate procedures to safeguard and manage assets.
- compliance with applicable laws and regulations and consistency with regulatory guidance.

---

[83] ATR standards may be found in 12 CFR 1026.51, "Ability to Pay"; 1026.43, "Minimum Standards for Transactions Secured by a Dwelling"; and 1026.34(a)(4), "Prohibited Acts or Practices in Connection with High-Cost Mortgages." Other relevant standards are found in 12 CFR 1026.32, "Requirements for High-Cost Mortgages."

[84] Refer to OCC Bulletin 2000-20, "Uniform Retail Credit Classification and Account Management Policy: Policy Implementation." Examiners may wish to use the "Uniform Retail Credit Classification and Account Management Policy Checklist," included as appendix D of this booklet.

[85] There are regulatory restrictions regarding the transferring, selling, or assigning of ownership rights for some retail lending products. For example, refer to 12 CFR 1026.43(e)(5)(ii) and 12 CFR 1026.43(f)(2). Refer also to footnote 84.

7. Assess whether clear and objective standards exist for identifying, approving, monitoring, and analyzing exceptions to policies and operating procedures. Consider whether policies address

   - board approval of policy exception processes.
   - identification, classification, and documentation of policy and operating procedure exceptions.
   - the approval process for exceptions, including escalation processes as the volume or significance increases.
   - monitoring, reporting, and analysis of policy exception volumes, performance, trends, and significance.
   - reporting of policy exceptions to the board, senior management, and applicable oversight committees.
   - periodic review of exceptions monitoring processes by independent control functions such as internal audit, external audit, or loan review.

Processes

Processes are the procedures, programs, and practices that impose order on a bank's pursuit of its objectives. Processes define how activities are carried out and help manage risk. Effective processes are consistent with the underlying policies and are governed by appropriate checks and balances (such as internal controls).

Objective: Evaluate whether risk appetite processes provide a sound foundation for business objectives and strategies.

1. Determine whether risk appetite development is supported by a thorough, systematic risk assessment exercise. Consider whether risk assessments

   - evaluate business strategies and objectives in the context of internal capabilities, the external environment, and available resources.
   - identify a broad range of important threats and risk events.
   - quantify potential exposures after consideration of likelihood and impact.
   - propose reasonable and appropriate contingency plans and responses.

2. Assess whether risk appetite statements support consistent risk decisions across the retail lending businesses. Consider whether risk appetite statements

   - are documented.
   - can be reconciled with the products and markets pursued by the bank.
   - are consistent with the bank's credit culture.
   - help define and provide context for relevant credit risks and drivers (concentrations, profitability, performance, etc.).
   - are supported by quantifiable measures (limits, triggers) established relative to bank-specific criteria such as portfolio composition, size, earnings, or capital.

- are considered during policy reviews and revisions, as well as for new products and portfolio acquisitions.
- are reassessed by the board and senior management at least annually, and whenever new business opportunities arise or risk capacity, operating environments, or other economic factors change.

3. Determine whether compliance with the established risk appetite is effectively monitored and managed by the board and senior management. Consider whether evidence suggests that

- risks are identified, aggregated, and considered within and across products, portfolios, and legal entities when measuring against risk tolerances.
- portfolio composition and performance can be reconciled to established risk appetites, allowing the board and senior management to track adherence.
- risk limits and escalation triggers exist at the overall retail portfolio level and for each significant product or product segment.
- risk levels are quantified and measured against tolerances and limits.
- processes exist to identify business units operating outside board-approved risk parameters, or not within the established risk appetite.
- the board receives periodic assessments of observed risk levels (and trends) to monitor compliance with the established risk appetite.

4. Evaluate whether retail business strategies are realistic, prudent, and consistent with the established risk appetite. Consider whether

- product and target-market strategies appear well conceived and practical.
- competitive analyses are comprehensive and realistic.
- consideration was given to current and expected economic conditions.
- marketing plans and budgets are consistent with business objectives.
- major assumptions are well defined and supported with critical analysis.
- the organizational structure, staffing levels, and business resources support any new initiatives or products.
- actual performance is regularly compared with established projections, plans, strategies, and initiatives.
- reports used to track performance are accurate, timely, and sufficiently detailed to promote informed evaluations and decisions.
- processes exist for amending the plans to reflect current information or trends.

Objective: Determine whether all significant retail credit processes receive proper oversight from the board and senior management.

1. Choose one or more credit processes (credit approvals, account management, collections, portfolio management, or independent control functions) and assess whether

- written policies, operating procedures, and process maps adequately govern each activity. Consider whether
  - policies, operating procedures, and process flows are appropriate for the size, complexity, and transaction volume of the product or activity.
  - a clear, complete, and complementary relationship exists between policies, operating procedures, and process maps.
  - documented procedures and process maps accurately reflect actual practices.
  - internal controls ensure that exceptions to policies, procedures, and limits are reported in a timely manner to the appropriate level of management.
  - internal audit or other independent control functions periodically test the accuracy and completeness of operating policies, procedures, and process maps.
  - an effective quality assurance or quality control process periodically confirms the effectiveness of significant controls and operating procedures.
- the board (or designated committee) approves all significant policies governing the area.
- oversight committees (credit or operating) have been established to support risk identification, risk assessment, and the open discussion of emerging issues. Consider whether committees have
  - broad participation by all parties important to the business or function.
  - regular meetings, with good attendance.
  - formal agendas and reports, provided in advance of the meetings so participants can prepare for discussions.
  - meeting minutes that document issues discussed, major decisions made, open issues, and follow-up responsibilities.
- compensation structures (especially incentive pay) are consistent with the established risk appetite and promote long-term, effective practices.
- effective processes promote consistent compliance with applicable laws and regulations. Consider whether
  - procedures are in place to comply with applicable laws and regulations.
  - processes exist to determine compliance with applicable laws and regulations.
  - reports to senior management and the board detail any concerns with compliance with applicable laws and regulations.
- an independent risk management function assesses risk and emerging issues for each activity on a regular basis.

Objective: Determine whether management reporting systems provide timely, accurate, and practical risk management information.

1. Determine whether the board and senior management have established effective management reporting as a bank-wide priority. Consider whether

- the board (or designated committee) periodically approves retail product policies and procedures that include management reporting standards appropriate for the volume, complexity, and risk profile of the products offered.

- meeting minutes from board and other oversight committees provide sufficient detail to follow the issues presented, topics discussed, decisions made, and required follow-up items or actions.
- independent control functions include the quality, depth, accuracy, and timing of management reporting as part of their normal scope of reviews.
- a quality assurance function periodically confirms the effectiveness of management reporting.
- reports to the board and senior management consistently
  - reflect the complexities and materiality of the bank's retail credit portfolio.
  - include a broad range of metrics, such as new transaction volumes, risk rating and other credit quality trends, industry and market concentrations, performance of loans granted as exceptions, emerging risks, loan pricing, and pipeline volumes.
  - identify significant assumptions, weaknesses, or limitations affecting the reliability of risk measures.
  - provide sufficient detail to promote timely, well-supported decisions.
  - focus on key metrics and trends in a format that is easy to understand and conveys complete, accurate, and timely details.
  - include summary narratives that provide substantive explanations and insight into changes and critical issues.
  - note the status of action items and issues, including those raised by regulators, auditors, credit audit, and credit review.
  - provide both high-level summaries and line-of-business results with the amount of detail commensurate with the audience and risk level.

2. Evaluate whether management reporting supports effective oversight of retail credit activities. Consider whether

   - reporting platforms for retail lending products are automated and integrated across the bank.
   - data on borrowers, portfolio segments, and products can be captured and aggregated to
     - provide accurate and reliable information for daily, monthly, and quarterly portfolio monitoring and management needs.
     - consolidate information across the retail-lending group, by business line, legal entity, product type, industry, region, and other groupings relevant to the risk.
     - meet ad hoc data requirements in response to emerging risks.
     - be incorporated appropriately into stress testing scenarios.
   - management reports regularly compare actual results with projections or other benchmarks to detect and address adverse trends or concerns in a timely manner. Peer bank information is presented for key metrics, such as loan growth, nonperforming assets, loan charge-offs, ALLL levels, and credit concentrations.
   - topics for standard retail management reports include
     - the level and trend of delinquencies, nonperforming and problem assets, charge-offs, weighted average risk ratings, and reserves in both balance sheet and off-balance-sheet accounts.

- – trends in growth, volume, and mix of retail lending and fee-based credit activities.
- – performance at the portfolio, product, and significant segment levels.
- – trends in loan pricing programs, portfolio analytics and models, loss forecasting, and stress testing.
- – monitoring of new originations volumes, performance, and credit quality versus the portfolio as a whole to support portfolio migration analysis.
- – trends in summary ratings assigned by independent control functions, such as risk management, internal audit, and retail loan review.
- – performance related to changes in underwriting standards and policy exceptions.
- – concentration levels and adherence to established risk limits.
- – trends and data supporting quarterly ALLL decisions.
- – emerging risks and actions taken to address those risks.
- • periodic reports provide an in-depth review of the portfolio in response to growth, changes in risk profile, new activities, or emerging risks to the bank or industry. Issues may be related to strategic or reputation risk that could affect retail credit.
- • annual presentations are made for specialized portfolios detailing overall risk profile, portfolio characteristics, strategy, and budgets.
- • key reports are periodically reconciled to source data for reliability.

Objective: Determine whether exception monitoring systems effectively identify, measure, monitor, and control credit-related policy and operating procedure noncompliance.

1. Determine whether processes for the identification, approval, management, and monitoring of policy exceptions are subject to prudent oversight. Consider whether

- • the board (or designated committee) periodically approves policies and procedures governing policy exception protocols for all significant retail credit activities.
- • exception guidelines clearly establish when and how exceptions may occur, and how each should be handled.
- • clear lines of responsibility and authority for identifying, approving, monitoring, and analyzing policy exceptions are established.
- • appropriate exception limits have been established.
- • exception monitoring policies and operating procedures are consistent with the board's established risk appetite and comprehensively define risk tolerance, responsibilities, and accountabilities.
- • management effectively assesses whether the exceptions policies, as applied, avoid discrimination on a prohibited basis in violation of fair lending laws (including the Equal Credit Opportunity Act, 15 USC 1691, and the Fair Housing Act, 42 USC 3605).
- • internal control processes exist for review of the exception-tracking process by an independent control function such as internal audit, external audit, or retail loan review.
- • a quality assurance function periodically reviews exception-handling processes.

2. Determine whether active management of policy exceptions occurs in each significant line of business or product. Consider whether

- the level, composition, and potential impact of exceptions for all significant activities are evaluated regularly. Determine if analysis considers
  - the level, trend, and performance of exceptions granted.
  - whether volumes conform to established limits, and whether those limits are reasonable.
  - the extent to which exceptions occur on new loans, renewals, and modifications.
  - whether certain exception types lead to higher default or loss rates, or weaker portfolio quality.
  - the impact of exception levels and trends on ALLL and capital adequacy.
- breaching an established exception threshold triggers more in-depth analysis and discussion.
- policy and exception levels and performance of loans with exceptions are considered when making changes to policy and underwriting guidelines.
- unidentified or material exception levels or failure to follow exception protocols are considered in employees' performance evaluations and compensation decisions.

3. Determine whether management reporting adequately supports exception-tracking activities for all retail lending products. Consider whether

- exception-tracking reports are timely, accurate, and complete and provide information needed for sound management and credible challenge.
- reporting systems capture and track exception information at the product, program, significant segment, and transaction levels.
- tracking reports compare actual exception levels with limits, projections, and/or qualitative benchmarks.
- tracking reports include the performance of loans with exceptions in the aggregate and by exception type, including loans with multiple exceptions.
- key management reports used to track policy exceptions are periodically validated and reconciled to source data to determine accuracy and reliability.
- reports to the board (or oversight committee) and senior management include an assessment of exceptions risk on an aggregate basis, including a dashboard of key measures relative to the approved risk appetite.

Objective: Determine whether credit approval processes operate in a structured, disciplined manner and promote compliance with applicable laws and regulations, including fair lending laws and regulations.

1. Choose one or more retail lending products and obtain an overview of the credit approval process. Document the process in the work papers, focusing on steps involved in application receipt and processing, credit decisions and approvals, and collateral valuation and lien perfection. Determine

- which aspects of the underwriting process are automated versus manual.
- what sources of information are used and required (credit bureaus, written applications, etc.).

- how loan amounts or credit line assignments are determined (use of matrixes, existence of collateral, etc.)
- where and how credit scores and scoring models are used (types of models, history of model use, monitoring, and validation).
- differences in the underwriting processes based on
  - products.
  - target markets (e.g., prime, near-prime, and subprime).
  - application channels (i.e., direct mail, telemarketing, Internet, and broker/dealer).
  - unsolicited versus pre-qualified or pre-approved applications.
- how security interests are perfected (who is responsible and how filings are completed and verified, etc.).
- whether insurance coverage is verified and continuously monitored.

2. Determine whether credit approval processes receive proper oversight from the board and senior management. Consider whether

- the board (or designated committee) approves all credit approval policies.
- written descriptions, flow charts, and process maps exist for the entire process, from application (or solicitation) through funding. Descriptions should fully explain all automated decision tools and judgmental decision points within the approval process.
- credit approval operating procedures provide for exception handling (e.g., identification, mitigation, reporting, and performance monitoring).
- risk management plays a definitive and clear role in establishing credit approval processes.
- oversight committees support risk identification, risk assessment, and open discussion of emerging issues.
- a qualified and independent party (e.g., internal audit, external audit, or retail loan review) regularly reviews credit approval processes.

3. Determine whether credit approval processes are compatible with the bank's credit culture, risk profile, and lender capabilities. Consider whether

- operating procedures and process maps provide clear guidance for
  - borrower selection criteria.
  - underwriting standards by market, industry, and product.
  - lending authorities and responsibilities.
  - loan amounts or credit line assignments.
  - handling policy exceptions.
  - credit quality thresholds and limits.
- consistent documentation standards are required and used for all credit approvals.
- credit approval documentation adequately supports credit decisions, including
  - transaction purpose.
  - loan terms.
  - loan amounts.
  - borrower financial information and analysis.
  - primary and secondary repayment sources.

– credit scores or risk ratings.
– collateral valuations.
– policy exceptions.
– other risk or reward considerations.

- compensation programs effectively balance revenue generation with the approved risk appetite. Compensation programs include a long-term component that incorporates credit quality results over time.
- ongoing training programs provide guidance on factors such as the bank's strategic goals, risk appetite metrics, policies and procedures, industry risk strategies, client selection criteria, underwriting standards, and risk mitigation strategies.

4. Determine whether brokers, correspondents, and other third-party loan originators are the subject of prudent due diligence and oversight. Assess whether

- an established framework exists for oversight of indirect lending activities and dealers.
- criteria exist for entering into, continuing, and exiting relationships with intermediaries and originators.
- loans purchased through a broker or intermediary reflect standards and practices consistent with those applied by the bank in its direct lending activities.
- internal processes and controls provide certainty that all purchased loans are consistent with the bank's underwriting criteria.
- contracts clearly specify credit criteria, loan documentation standards, collateral valuation requirements, reporting requirements, quality control reviews, and other methods that allow the bank to verify compliance with agreements, bank policies, and laws and regulations.
- compensation to third parties is structured to avoid providing incentives to originate loans with predatory or abusive characteristics (for example, through the use of maximum rates, points, and other charges, and the use of overages and yield-spread premiums), and complies with applicable regulations.[86]
- each new third party is subject to defined due diligence before establishing a relationship.
- independent control functions in the bank, such as risk management, internal audit, and loan review, include indirect lending activities as part of normal oversight scope and reviews.

5. Evaluate whether retail loan structures support disciplined lending and orderly debt repayment. Consider whether

- loan terms display a prudent consistency with the loan purpose, expected source of repayment, timing of repayment, and the value and useful life of any collateral pledged.

---

[86] With respect to closed-end mortgages, refer to 12 CFR 1026.36, "Prohibited Acts or Practices and Certain Requirements for Credit Secured by a Dwelling" (related to loan originator compensation and steering).

- loan terms are consistent with the nature of markets and lending environments involved.
- required minimum payments and amortization schedules
  - provide regular and ongoing contact with the borrower.
  - permit the borrower to demonstrate (and the bank to assess) ongoing ability to repay outstanding amounts in a structured, orderly manner.
  - are consistent with the borrower's documented creditworthiness.
  - are consistent with the loan purpose.
  - minimize the deferral of principal or interest, and prevent prolonged negative amortization.
- loan pricing is a risk-based consideration of the borrower's financial condition, loan terms and amortization schedules, and the current and projected value of any collateral pledged.

6. Assess whether credit lines for revolving products are assigned using prudent credit criteria. Consider whether

- initial line assignments and line increases adequately consider the borrower's repayment capacity.
- line assignment and line increase criteria are part of a structured, documented process that includes testing and analysis before broad implementation.
- debt service capacity evaluations consider the borrower's ability to repay at least the full minimum required payment on a fully drawn line.
- documentation for credit line assignments includes support and analysis of decision factors such as prior history, risk scores, behavior scores, and other relevant criteria.
- multiple credit lines to a single borrower are controlled and monitored.

7. Determine whether over-limit approvals for revolving lines of credit are reasonable and controlled.[87] Consider whether over-limit practices

- operate within defined policies and controls, including borrower eligibility, authorization buffer amounts, and repayment expectations.
- restrict over-limit authorizations for higher-risk accounts.
- require timely repayment of amounts exceeding established credit limits.
- are supported by management reporting with the ability to effectively identify, measure, manage, and control exposures.

8. Evaluate whether credit decisions for each retail product appropriately consider both the capacity and the willingness of the borrower to repay the debt as agreed. Consider whether decision processes

---

[87] For credit card accounts, assess the bank's implementation of the over-limit guidance in OCC Bulletin 2003-1, "Credit Card Lending: Account Management and Loss Allowance Guidance." Refer to appendix E, "Account Management and Loss Allowance Guidance Checklist," of this booklet. Also refer to 12 CFR 1026.56, "Requirements for Over-the-Limit Transactions," for opt-in requirements.

- operate within defined measurement criteria and documentation requirements.
- evaluate the borrower's overall financial condition and resources.
- evaluate the borrower's financial capacity to repay the subject loan in full, under the terms and conditions of the loan agreement.
- consider the borrower's character and willingness to repay as agreed.
- consider the financial capability and responsibility of any guarantor or insurance provider.
- evaluate the nature and value of any underlying collateral.

9. Determine whether effective processes govern the acceptability, valuation, and perfection of collateral.[88] Consider whether

- collateral-related policies and procedures are consistent with the established risk appetite, transaction types, and complexity of the products offered.
- collateral valuations are performed by qualified individuals independent of the credit approval process.
- collateral valuation standards define
  - appropriate approaches to valuation by product and transaction type.
  - methods for reconciling differences in value estimates.
  - required valuation updates when a material change in the borrower's risk profile or market conditions occurs.
  - supporting documentation requirements that include a description of assumptions and the basis for the value estimate.
  - valuation documentation to be reviewed before credit approval.
- management reporting systems support collateral activities, and are appropriate for the size and complexity of transactions.
- independent control function(s) (such as internal audit, external audit, or retail loan review) review collateral valuation activities.
- a quality assurance program periodically confirms the effectiveness of controls over collateral valuation activities.

10. Evaluate the adequacy of the process for changing credit approval standards. Review all changes in policies and significant operating procedures since the last examination, and determine their effect on quality or risk trends in the loan portfolio.

---

[88] National banks and federal savings associations are required under 12 CFR 34, subpart D, and 12 CFR 160.101, respectively, to adopt and maintain written real estate lending policies. Pursuant to 12 CFR 34, subpart D, appendix A, "Interagency Guidelines for Real Estate Lending," these policies should include a real estate appraisal and evaluation program. Such programs are designed to ensure that reliable appraisals and evaluations are obtained when required under 12 CFR 34, subpart C. Additionally, in 2010, the bank regulatory agencies published the "Interagency Appraisal and Evaluation Guidelines." (Refer to OCC Bulletin 2010-42, "Sound Practices for Appraisals and Evaluations: Interagency Appraisal and Evaluation Guidelines.") These guidelines describe the elements of a sound program for conducting appraisals and evaluations to support real estate-related financial transactions. Refer to the "Residential Real Estate Lending" booklet of the *Comptroller's Handbook* for more information on collateral valuation standards for residential real estate.

- Review analyses and documentation supporting recent changes to credit approval criteria (e.g., credit score cut-offs, collateral advance rates, cash reserves, maximum debt-to-income ratios).
- Discuss reasons for changes (if not readily apparent) with bank management and determine whether there was a shift in the credit risk appetite.
- Determine whether all affected functional areas provide input to the department making credit approval changes.
- Verify that management maintains a chronology of significant changes to credit approval processes and credit approval standards.

Objective: Determine whether originate-to-sell activities operate in a structured, disciplined manner.[89]

1. Determine whether originate-to-sell programs receive proper oversight from the board and senior management. Consider whether

- originate-to-sell programs operate under board-approved policies.
- policies and operating procedures are consistent with the established risk appetite and provide comprehensive definitions of risk tolerance, responsibilities, and accountabilities.
- effective processes exist for identifying, approving, monitoring, and reporting exceptions to established policies and operating procedures.
- originate-to-sell activities fall within the scope of an independent control function's review, such as internal audit, external audit, or loan review.

2. Determine whether originate-to-sell activities are compatible with the bank's credit culture, its risk profile, and the capabilities of its lenders. Consider whether

- business strategies define originate-to-sell program goals and objectives.
- written originate-to-sell policies and operating procedures specify
    - industry, client, and product selection criteria.
    - underwriting standards by market, industry, and product.
    - hedging requirements and underlying controls.
    - limit structures for pipeline production.
- exposure limits are used to manage concentrations by product types, economic sectors, and geographic areas.
- controls restrict the holding period for stale inventory, requiring managers to document action plans and disposition time frames.
- price and structural flexibility is frequently used to respond to evolving market conditions.
- sell-down strategies are explicit and consistently documented.
- program managers and the treasury funding desk communicate regularly to manage liquidity and funding options.

---

[89] Note that some regulatory requirements may limit such activities. For more information, refer to 12 CFR 1026.43(e)(5) and (f)(2), "Minimum Standards for Transactions Secured by a Dwelling."

- repurchase exposures are monitored and adequate reserves are maintained.
- economic or regulatory capital is allocated at the time of legal commitment.

3. Determine whether management reporting effectively supports originate-to-sell oversight, management, and monitoring. Consider whether

- management reports routinely
  - compare actual results with projections or other benchmarks.
  - present current and anticipated positions against limits.
  - show profit and losses on significant segments and the aggregate originate-to-sell program.
- pipeline reports show expected and stressed-loss earnings, stratified exposures by region, line of business, and industry, and sell-down assessments (i.e., easy, moderate, difficult) for each significant segment.
- key reports are periodically validated and reconciled to source data.

Objective: Determine whether new products or significant initiatives are subject to prudent due diligence (including an assessment of the requirements to comply with applicable laws and regulations), controls, and testing before broad adoption.

1. Determine whether prudent oversight for new products or significant initiatives exists. Evaluate whether

- new products or significant initiatives are approved in advance by the board or an appropriate board committee.
- "significant" has been reasonably defined and documented.
- new products or significant initiatives fall within the realm of oversight committees that support risk identification and risk assessment and provide an active forum to discuss emerging issues.
- new-product or significant initiative strategies and objectives are reviewed for consistency with the established risk appetite.
- policies and operating procedures are consistent with the size, volume, and desired risk profile of new products or significant initiatives.
- new-product or significant initiative internal control processes are subject to review by an independent control function such as risk management, internal audit, external audit, or loan review.
- quality assurance reviews periodically confirm the effectiveness of internal controls for new products or significant initiatives.

2. Assess whether due diligence for new products or significant initiatives includes

- evaluating how the proposed product or initiative fits with the existing business strategy and risk profile.
- input from all important affected areas (credit, funding, compliance, operations, control functions, etc.) regarding potential business impacts or concerns.

- assessing the resources needed to effectively manage the product or significant initiative, including the need to acquire additional expertise.
- developing viable alternatives, including an exit strategy, in case the product or significant initiative fails to perform as expected.

3. Determine whether all new products or significant initiatives are subject to testing before broad implementation.[90] Consider whether product tests

- are required for all new products or significant initiatives.
- define test objectives, methods (e.g., assumptions, test size, selection criteria, and duration), and key performance measures in advance.
- include a holdout group that is not subject to other significant account management or cross-selling initiatives for the duration of the test.
- include test periods long enough to determine probable performance and to work through operational or other issues.
- design and test monitoring reports before test rollout.
- have defined approval processes based on the size, importance, and potential impact of the product or significant initiative.

4. Assess whether the bank conducts adequate due diligence on third-party relationships used for new products or significant initiatives. Consider whether

- due diligence includes assessing the third party's reputation, products, financial condition, and information security audit results.
- the bank has an ongoing oversight program to monitor the third party's activities.
- the bank has a contingency plan in case the third party cannot perform as expected.

5. Assess whether new products or significant initiatives are monitored after initial tests to compare actual with expected performance. Consider whether

- volumes and performance are monitored separately for a defined period after rollout.
- initial tests identified specific objectives and performance criteria for evaluating success.
- follow-up monitoring includes triggers or guardrails prompting further analysis or actions if actual results are significantly below or above expectations.

6. Assess whether internal controls for new products or significant initiatives include

- expanding and amending bank policies and procedures.
- including parameters in policies and procedures that establish accountability and provide for exception monitoring.
- implementing reporting systems to monitor adherence to objectives and limits.

---

[90] Refer to OCC Bulletin 2004-20, "Risk Management of New, Expanded, or Modified Bank Products and Services: Risk Management Process," for national banks, and *OTS Examination Handbook*, section 760, "New Activities and Services," for federal savings associations.

- developing monitoring reports with key indicators to effectively identify, measure, monitor, and control risk.
- incorporating the product or initiative into the bank's audit and compliance processes.

Objective: Assess processes for the design and implementation of account management programs and activities for retail credit accounts.

1. Determine whether account management programs and activities receive proper oversight from the board and senior management. Consider whether

    - the board (or designated committee) periodically approves policies and significant account management strategies before implementation.
    - account management policies and operating procedures are consistent with the established risk appetite.
    - major strategies and initiatives are subject to testing before full rollout or widespread use.
    - exceptions to established policies and operating procedures are actively identified, monitored, and evaluated.
    - approval and escalation processes are in place to handle significant exceptions to policies or risk limits.
    - an independent control function such as internal audit, external audit, or retail loan review includes account management programs and activities within its normal scope of operations.
    - quality assurance reviews periodically evaluate and confirm the effectiveness of account management programs and actions.

2. Determine whether account management strategies are developed in a sound and prudent manner. Consider whether

    - strategy approvals include all relevant units (e.g., risk management, marketing, customer service, compliance, information technology, and finance).
    - new strategies consider the potential effects on credit performance, attrition, adverse retention, earnings, compliance, and the bank's reputation.
    - due diligence properly considers the impact of overlapping or repeat strategies.
    - testing occurs before full implementation for strategies with potential for significant credit or earnings impact.
    - program objectives and monitoring reports are developed before strategy testing begins.
    - tests run long enough to obtain reasonable results on performance and impact.
    - management regularly monitors and analyzes actual versus expected results during testing and for an appropriate period after rollout.
    - management responds promptly to both positive and negative performance differing from expectations.

3. Evaluate whether account management practices are consistent with prudent risk management and applicable regulatory guidance.[91] Determine whether

- transaction authorizations (approvals, holds, and denials) are well defined and controlled. Consider
  - how the bank establishes transaction limits and over-limit buffers (e.g., dollar amount, frequency, and cash versus purchase allocations).
  - criteria used to freeze accounts or prohibit additional transactions.
  - how the bank controls the types and volumes of transactions likely to circumvent the bank's authorization process (e.g., small dollar transactions, recurring transactions, delayed postings).
  - processes for handling payments returned for insufficient funds and large payment holds.
- credit line increase, decrease, and suspension actions are structured and controlled. Consider whether programs and initiatives are
  - subject to specific strategies and eligibility criteria.
  - part of designed strategies appropriately tested and evaluated before widespread use.
  - subject to comprehensive reporting providing data on volume, trends, and performance of accounts granted line increases, decreases, or suspensions.
  - consistently managed within authorization buffers, account terms, and conditions for repaying over-limit balances.
- the assessment and waiving of late, over-limit, extension, annual, and other fees are well managed and controlled. Determine whether
  - policies and operating procedures provide practical guidance for permissible actions.
  - practices are consistent with established guidelines.
  - the effect on account performance is adequately monitored and analyzed.
- explicit standards control the use of re-ages for open-end accounts.[92] Assess whether standards require appropriate controls, such as
  - a demonstrated and renewed willingness and ability to repay the loan.
  - a requirement that an account must have been open for at least nine months.
  - at least three consecutive minimum monthly payments or the equivalent cumulative amount before re-aging.
  - limits on re-ages to one in the prior 12 months, or two in any five-year period (except for a one-time permissible workout re-age).

---

[91] The primary regulatory guidelines relating to retail credit account management activities can be found in OCC Bulletin 2000-20, "Uniform Retail Credit Classification and Account Management Policy: Policy Implementation," and OCC Bulletin 2003-1, "Credit Card Lending: Account Management and Loss Allowance Guidance." Other guidelines, including standards in the Credit Card Accountability Responsibility and Disclosure Act, a 2009 amendment to the Truth in Lending Act, and Regulation B, which implements the Equal Credit Opportunity Act, may also apply. Mortgage servicing rules may also apply. For more information, refer to the "Truth in Lending Act," Real Estate Settlement Procedures Act," "Credit Card Lending," and "Fair Lending" booklets of the *Comptroller's Handbook*.

[92] These standards should be consistent with OCC Bulletin 2000-20, "Uniform Retail Credit Classification and Account Management Policy: Policy Implementation."

- explicit standards control the use of extensions, deferrals, renewals, and rewrites for closed-end loans. Consider whether
  - borrowers are expected to demonstrate a renewed willingness and ability to repay the loan.
  - policies specifically limit the number and frequency of extensions, deferrals, renewals, and rewrites.
  - policies prohibit advances to finance unpaid interest and fees.

4. Determine whether management reporting systems effectively support account management activities. Consider whether

   - reporting systems for account management activities can
     - aggregate an entire loan relationship by customer (multiple loan accounts by product and in total).
     - identify and document any loan that is re-aged, extended, deferred, renewed, or re-written, including the number of times any action was taken.
     - monitor and track the volume and performance of loans re-aged, extended, deferred, renewed, or rewritten or placed in a workout program.
     - compare actual results with projections or other benchmarks to detect and address adverse trends or concerns.
     - document that bank personnel communicated with the borrower, the borrower agreed to pay the loan in full, and the borrower has the ability to repay the loan.
   - key reports are periodically reconciled with source data to determine accuracy and reliability.
   - reports to the board (or other oversight committee) and senior management include a clear assessment of account management risk on an aggregate basis, including a dashboard report of key measures relative to the approved risk appetite.

Objective: Determine whether collections and workout program processes operate in a structured, disciplined manner.

1. Evaluate whether collections and workout activities are subject to proper oversight. Consider whether

   - the board (or designated committee) approves policies and significant collections and workout program strategies before implementation.
   - collections and workout program policies and operating procedures are consistent with the established risk appetite.
   - major collections and workout strategies and initiatives are subject to appropriate testing before full rollout or widespread use.
   - exceptions to established policies and operating procedures are actively identified, monitored, and evaluated.
   - approval and escalation processes exist to handle exceptions to policy, concentration, or other risk limits.

- an independent control function such as internal audit, external audit, or retail loan review includes collections and workout program activities (including adherence to applicable regulatory guidance) within its normal scope of operations.
- quality assurance reviews periodically evaluate and determine the effectiveness of collections and workout program processes.

2. Evaluate whether established processes result in the efficient and effective transfer of problem credits to collections departments or workout specialists. Consider whether

- collections staff expertise aligns with the complexity of the bank's products, risk profile, and target markets.
- objective standards exist for transferring retail accounts to collections departments or workout specialists.
- operating procedures for initial transfer to collections or workout specialists include requirements for
    - determining whether loan documents were properly executed, collateral was properly perfected, and any loan or collateral documentation exceptions are corrected.
    - evaluating the borrower's current financial condition, cause of financial problems, external factors that may affect their ability to repay, and any reputation risks associated with the borrower or product type.
    - obtaining collateral valuations for collections accounts that are based on market value from independent and knowledgeable sources.
    - applying proper accounting standards for issues such as troubled debt restructurings (TDR), loan modifications, or income accrual.
- credit files (or collections systems) document current exposure; the history leading to the problem situation; trends and key issues (including legal); financial metrics; collateral values; workout strategies and action plans; and the potential for nonaccrual or loss.
- post-mortem evaluations of problem assets are periodically performed to identify causes, evaluate collections strategies, and determine whether underwriting standards need revision.

3. Determine whether appropriate processes govern the development and implementation of collections strategies and workout programs. Consider whether

- responsibilities for strategy development are assigned to a specific person or group.
- proposed workout strategies require projections or performance thresholds to aid in evaluating whether treatments are performing within expected ranges, and identifying the need for adjustments.
- placement in a workout program (temporary or permanent) relates directly to the nature, severity, and expected duration of each borrower's hardship or specific circumstances.
- workout strategies for each borrower include a cost-benefit analysis of retention versus exit considering all available options.

- payment terms for borrowers in temporary workout programs are consistent with the nature of the hardship and restoring the borrower to non-problem status.
- payment terms for borrowers in permanent workout programs focus on ensuring the bank recovers principal amounts as quickly and efficiently as possible.
- proper testing (test size, time frames, account population, and characteristics) occurs before expanding new workout programs or strategies.
- the testing process accumulates sufficient data to measure strategy success and make informed decisions.
- change logs are maintained for each workout program or collections strategy to support ongoing analysis and decisions.
- the bank has a formal process to periodically assess the efficiency and effectiveness of the full range of workout strategies available to the collections department or workout specialists.
- successes and failures are documented and retained to help inform future proposals.

4. Evaluate the consistency of the bank's retail loan classifications (including charge-offs), re-ages, extensions, deferrals, renewals, rewrites, and internal or external workout programs with regulatory and accounting guidance.

- Compare the bank's collection and workout-area policies and operating procedures with the criteria in
  - the "Uniform Retail Credit Classification and Account Management Policy Checklist," included as appendix D of this booklet.
  - workout and forbearance practices included in the "Account Management and Loss Allowance Checklist," included as appendix E of this booklet.
- Determine where management has implemented automated versus manual processes to follow regulatory and accounting guidelines for loan classifications.
  - If automated, review the system settings to verify that the parameters correspond to those described in the bank's policies and regulatory guidelines.
  - If manual, review the operating procedures used to determine whether loans are likely to receive appropriate classifications in a systematic and methodical manner.
- If the bank does not place severely delinquent retail and residential real estate loans on nonaccrual, identify the methods the bank employs to accurately measure income and determine that it is not materially overstated (e.g., loss allowances for uncollectible fees and finance charges).
- Request a report detailing retail loans by product that reached 90 days past due during the previous quarter. Confirm that each was classified substandard and included in management reports of classified loans.
- Determine whether losses are automatically or manually processed, any circumstances possibly delaying a charge-off, and when the bank recognizes losses (i.e., daily, weekly, or monthly). Determine how accounts scheduled for charge-off are loaded into a charge-off queue or other system for loss.
- Request a report detailing closed-end accounts more than 120 days past due and open-end accounts more than 180 days past due that are not charged off or, if secured, written down to the value of collateral, less cost to sell. Review the report with

management, and determine why those balances remain on the bank's books and whether there are system or policy issues needing correction.

5. Assess whether appropriate processes control the use of third parties used to collect delinquent accounts or recover losses, such as debt buyers, skip tracers, repossession agents, and legal firms. Consider whether

   - responsibility and authority for managing third-party collections agencies lie with a specific individual.
   - a formal due diligence process is used to select third-party collections agencies.
   - contracts and proposed collections practices are reviewed by the applicable risk personnel, such as the bank's legal counsel and compliance officer.
   - contracts include well-defined performance tolerances and termination requirements.
   - regular monitoring compares third-party performance to established performance tolerances and contractual provisions.
   - a defined process allocates accounts between internal collections and third-party collections agencies.
   - productivity reports, amounts collected, and fees disbursed are reviewed regularly for each third-party collections agency.
   - third-party collections agencies are subject to periodic reviews by an independent control function such as internal audit, external audit, retail loan review, or quality assurance.

6. Evaluate whether appropriate processes control the handling of fraudulent accounts. Consider whether

   - fraudulent accounts are charged off within 90 days of discovery.
   - fraud is well-defined and fraud losses are appropriately distinguished from credit losses.
   - fraud losses are recognized as operating expenses rather than charges to the ALLL.
   - policies and procedures differentiate between an allegedly fraudulent amount in an account versus an undisputed amount.
   - when investigation negates the fraud allegation, the bank returns accounts to the previous delinquency status and immediately reinstates collection efforts.

7. Determine whether management reporting systems effectively support collections and workout program activities. Consider whether

   - reporting systems for collections and workout program activities can
     - aggregate an entire loan relationship by customer (multiple loan accounts by product and in total).
     - provide asset-level detail for each account assigned to the collections department or any workout program.
     - monitor and track the volume and performance of individual loans assigned to collections or enrolled in any temporary or permanent workout program.

- monitor and track the volumes, performance, and success rates of collections strategies and workout programs.
- provide trends on activity, volumes, and performance for collections as a whole, and for each individual strategy or workout program.
- compare actual results with projections or qualitative benchmarks for collections as a whole, and any individual strategies or workout programs.
- document account activity, history, and communications with the borrower through any aspect of collections or workout program activities.
- identify and monitor accounts with exceptions to collections or workout program policies and operating procedures.
- collections systems adequately document borrower interaction before enrollment in a temporary or permanent workout program. Documentation shows
  - the nature of the hardship or problem.
  - any scheduled follow-up actions if the issue causing the borrower's difficulties is not resolved.
  - the borrower has committed to making workout program payments.
  - why the bank expects the borrower to be able to make the workout program payments assigned.
- key reports are periodically reconciled with source data to determine accuracy and reliability.
- reports to the board (or other oversight committee) and senior management include a clear assessment of collections and workout program risk on an aggregate basis, including a dashboard report of key measures relative to the approved risk appetite.

Objective: Determine whether risk identification and portfolio management activities operate in a structured, disciplined manner.

1. Determine whether credit quality monitoring processes receive proper oversight from the board and senior management. Consider whether

   - the board (or a designated committee) periodically approves policies and procedures specific to risk identification and performance monitoring that are appropriate for the bank's risk profile and complexity of the products and loan structures offered.
   - risk identification policies and operating procedures are consistent with the board's established risk appetite and comprehensively define risk tolerance, responsibilities, and accountabilities.
   - risk identification and performance monitoring policies and procedures include standards and guidelines for handling exceptions to policies and operating procedures (identification, mitigation, reporting, and performance monitoring).
   - an independent control function such as internal audit, external audit, or retail loan review regularly evaluates control systems and policy adherence related to risk identification and performance monitoring.
   - a quality assurance function periodically confirms the effectiveness of risk identification and performance monitoring controls.

2. Determine whether borrower risk-identification and loan performance monitoring are a high priority and operates in accordance with approved guidelines.[93] Consider whether

- credit quality is monitored continuously at the individual borrower, significant segment, product, and portfolio levels.
- monitoring activities operate as an important early warning system, allowing credit issues or credit deterioration to be elevated in a timely and effective manner.
- the level of attention and monitoring is proportional to the inherent credit risk (at the borrower, segment, product, or portfolio level).
- business and risk managers have experience and expertise with the products offered, and can properly identify and respond to changing risk levels.
- loan products with extended maturities or principal deferral (e.g., loans with interest-only monthly payments) do not rely solely on delinquency performance to monitor borrower quality and financial condition.
- collateral valuation updates occur as appropriate based on borrower ratings, exposure levels, and industry issues.
- guidelines specify when independent third-party valuations, inspections, and audits of collateral are required.
- borrower, portfolio, and product monitoring activities are influenced by industry or concentration risk. The bank uses internal and external sources as early warning triggers to identify potential areas of concern.
- changes in economic conditions are an explicit factor when assessing portfolio condition, account management initiatives, and collections activities.

3. Determine whether management reporting supports active and effective risk identification and credit quality monitoring. Consider whether

- reporting platforms used for risk identification and performance monitoring are automated and integrated across the bank.
- management reports
  - are complete and aggregate relevant risks across the organization.
  - are accurate and timely.
  - provide information needed for sound management and credible challenge.
  - compare actual results with projections and qualitative benchmarks to add perspective and detect and address adverse trends or concerns in a timely manner.
  - include performance metrics associated with the approved risk appetite that are available and tracked regularly.
- key borrower quality and performance monitoring reports are periodically validated and reconciled to source data, ensuring reliability.
- reports to the board (or other oversight committee) and senior management include a clear assessment of risk levels and credit performance on an aggregate basis, including a dashboard report of key measures relative to the approved risk appetite.

---

[93] Examiners should ensure that the bank has sufficient policies and operating procedures to identify and address consumer protection, fair lending, and BSA/AML risks. Any identified consumer compliance concerns may require subsequent supervisory activities.

4. Determine whether management of retail credit concentrations receives proper oversight from the board and senior management. Consider whether

- the board (or a designated committee) periodically approves policies and procedures for identifying and managing concentrations appropriate for the retail credit portfolio's size, risk profile, and complexity.
- concentration management policies and operating procedures are consistent with the board's established risk appetite and comprehensively define risk tolerance, responsibilities, and accountabilities.
- credit concentration limits are established and managed for retail lending as a whole, and for each significant product.
- concentration limits are well defined, well communicated, and consistently applied across retail lending products and portfolios.
- concentration management policies and procedures include standards and guidelines for handling exceptions to policies and operating procedures (identification, mitigation, reporting, and performance monitoring).
- an independent control function such as internal audit, external audit, or retail loan review regularly evaluates internal controls and policy adherence related to concentrations risk management.
- a quality assurance function periodically confirms the effectiveness of concentration limit controls.

5. Determine whether risk and concentration limits are established and managed in a prudent manner. Consider whether

- a company-wide framework identifies retail credit concentrations and correlated exposures across business lines, including bulk loan purchases and asset-backed securities for the applicable asset classes.
- credit concentration limits are well defined and actively monitored.
- exposures to higher-risk products or borrower segments are generally subject to lower exposure limits.
- management expertise in various products or markets is considered when establishing risk limits.
- exposure limits are dynamic and based on current positions, market trends, and industry conditions.
- notional limits are supplemented with risk-based credit equivalents (e.g., economic capital and loan equivalent exposures).
- credit concentrations nearing or exceeding approved limits are subject to enhanced review and reporting.
- a formal process identifies and escalates exposures approaching or exceeding approved concentration and risk limits.
- established risk mitigation strategies, tools, or activities are used to manage significant credit concentrations (e.g., loan sales, securitization, curtailment, and derivatives).

- risk mitigants (e.g., collateral, protection sellers, and guarantors) are regularly monitored and evaluated for effectiveness at the transaction and portfolio levels.
- formal evaluations of high-risk retail credit concentrations are conducted periodically.
- portfolio-level and specific stress testing is used to identify potential credit concentrations and assess their impact on the bank's asset quality, earnings, capital and liquidity.

6. Determine whether management reporting systems support active and effective oversight of risk and concentration limit management. Consider whether

- reporting systems adequately support the size, risk profile, and complexity of the retail portfolio.
- reporting platforms are automated and integrated across the bank.
- concentration-related management reports
  - are complete and aggregate relevant risks across the bank.
  - are accurate and timely.
  - provide information needed for sound management and credible challenge.
  - compare actual results with projections and qualitative benchmarks to add perspective and detect adverse trends or concerns in a timely manner.
  - include limits-related performance metrics associated with the approved risk appetite.
- a tracking mechanism monitors the effectiveness of hedging activity and determines the appropriate time to close out positions. Justifications for closing positions are clearly documented and forwarded to the applicable (e.g., credit or enterprise risk) committee.
- potential issues or risks related to the types of hedging employed are communicated to the board (or designated committee).
- key reports are periodically validated and reconciled to source data to ensure reliability.
- reports to the board (or other oversight committee) and senior management include a clear assessment of concentration risk on an aggregate basis, including a dashboard report of key measures relative to the approved risk appetite.

7. Determine whether borrower segmentation systems are appropriate for the nature, size, and complexity of the bank's retail product types, borrower base, and payment structures.[94] Consider whether

- the ratings system includes an appropriate number of grades (or segments) that result in a meaningful distribution of exposures that supports active risk analysis and management.

---

[94] Some smaller community banks with non-complex retail portfolios may use delinquency-based ratings or segmentation systems, or only the regulatory risk classifications for retail credit described in OCC Bulletin 2000-20, "Uniform Retail Credit Classification and Account Management Policy: Policy Implementation." Banks with larger, or more complex retail portfolios should have more robust ratings or segmentation systems.

- ratings and segmentation criteria are written, clear, and consistently applied, and include specific factors for assigning classification.
- all consumer exposures have ratings or segment assignments, except for approved exceptions.
- rating or segmentation assignments are dynamic, with changes based on variations in a borrower's risk profile.
- ratings and segment assignments are reviewed and updated whenever new material information is received, but not less than annually.
- exceptions to specified ratings or segmentation criteria are rare. Procedures for overrides or omissions are well defined. Overrides (judgmental or policy) or omissions are identified, analyzed, and monitored to evaluate the impact on the risk rating system.
- independent validation processes confirm and assure the accuracy of risk rating or segmentation systems on an ongoing basis.
- risk rating and segmentation reports provide a clear assessment of portfolio mix and composition by significant segment and product and on an aggregate basis, including a dashboard of key measurements relative to the approved risk appetite.
- add-on products (debt suspension, debt cancellation, credit life, skip-a-pay, etc.) are managed prudently and do not distort credit quality evaluations or analysis.
- a quality assurance function periodically confirms the effectiveness of the risk rating and segmentation systems.

8. Assess whether stress testing for retail portfolios is appropriate for the size, risk profile, and complexity of the products offered. Consider whether

- the retail credit stress-testing framework is fully integrated within the retail business and other decision-making functions.
- stress events are designed to identify the impact on asset quality, earnings, capital, and liquidity.
- stress-test characteristics include that
  - the complexity of any given test does not undermine its integrity, usefulness, or clarity.
  - testing relies on high-quality, readily available input data and information to produce credible outcomes.
  - assumptions and the degree of uncertainty of inputs to the stress tests are documented.
  - testing looks beyond assumptions based only on historical data and challenges conventional assumptions.
  - testing is conducted over various time horizons, including the life of the loan exposures, to adequately capture both conditions that may materialize in the near term and adverse situations that take longer to develop.
  - testing development is iterative, with ongoing adjustments and refinements to better calibrate the tests to provide current and relevant information.
- stress tests are tailored to, and specifically capture, the retail business's exposures, activities, and risks. Exercises include

- the potential impact of adverse outcomes, such as an economic downturn or declining asset values.
  - scenarios relevant to the direction and strategy set by the board.
  - scenarios sufficiently severe to be credible to internal and external stakeholders.
- whether exposures, activities, and risks under normal and stressed conditions are aligned with the approved risk appetite.
- stress test results are clear, actionable, and well supported, providing for informed decision-making. Consider whether
  - results are accompanied by descriptive and qualitative information (such as key assumptions and limitations) allowing users to interpret the exercises in context.
  - results foster dialogue, keep the board (or designated committee), senior management, and staff apprised, and inform stress testing approaches, results, and decisions in other areas of the bank.
  - benchmarking or other comparative analysis is used to provide proper context and a check on results.
- validation or other types of independent reviews consistent with supervisory expectations are used to ensure process integrity and results.

Objective: Determine whether the process for establishing the ALLL is well defined and objective, and clearly supports the adequacy of current reserve levels.

1. Determine whether activities to establish the allowance for retail lending products receives appropriate board and senior management oversight. Consider whether

   - the board periodically approves allowance policies and procedures appropriate for the size and complexity of the retail credit products offered.
   - the board (or a designated committee) provides active oversight for the ALLL process and controls, reviewing recommendations and approving appropriate levels for the ALLL.
   - adequate resources are allocated to support the depth and level of analysis necessary given the current risk profile and portfolio complexity.
   - changes to the process are properly discussed, approved, and documented.
   - an independent control function such as internal audit, external audit, or retail loan review periodically reviews the loan-loss allowance process.
   - an independent quality assurance framework is in place to confirm the effectiveness of the allowance process.

2. Evaluate ALLL practices relative to retail lending. Consider whether

   - analysis includes all pertinent information existing as of the financial statement date, including environmental factors such as industry, geographical, economic, and political factors.
   - methodology results are consistent with the quality of the portfolio, economic conditions, and regulatory and accounting requirements.

- the ALLL process includes the opportunity for qualified parties (risk managers, oversight committee members, etc.) to provide credible challenge to qualitative and economic assumptions.
- changes to the portfolio affecting inherent losses are analyzed and incorporated into the process in a timely manner. This includes new products, acquisitions, or trends that affect asset quality and ultimately inherent losses.
- periodic validation of the bank's ALLL methodology and its application are performed by a party independent of the credit approval and ALLL estimation processes.
- back-testing of results is performed periodically for both the ASC 310-10, "Receivables," and ASC 450-20, "Contingencies," portions of the ALLL.
- the quarterly ALLL adequacy package provides well-documented and comprehensive support for the bank's decisions.
- loss estimation processes in place are consistent with GAAP.
- inherent losses for off-balance-sheet exposures are analyzed appropriately, but included in a separate liability account on the bank's balance sheet.

3. Assess whether the ALLL is established following ASC 310-10 for retail loans individually evaluated for impairment. Consider whether

- the process for identifying impaired loans is clear and consistently applied. Selection criteria can include loans based on exposure size, risk rating, delinquency, nonaccrual status, or other relevant criteria.
- determination of impairment status (i.e., impaired or not impaired) is well supported.
- measured impairment amounts are fully supported and documented based on one of the three appropriate methods: present value of expected cash flows, fair value of collateral less cost to sell (only when a loan is collateral dependent), or observable market price when a market exists.
- documentation for the impairment measurement method used, sources of information, as well as calculations, adjustments, and other assumptions are transparent and can be understood by others not familiar with the credit.
- policy or procedure guidance includes a clear, understandable definition of when a loan is considered collateral dependent, and such guidance is in accordance with GAAP and consistent with supervisory guidance.
- the bank properly accounts for any portion of the fair value of the recorded investment in a collateral-dependent loan in excess of the fair value of the collateral.
- loans below established thresholds are grouped with other loans sharing common characteristics, as appropriate.
- all TDRs are evaluated for impairment; however, TDRs below established thresholds and performing TDRs may be grouped with other loans sharing common characteristics.
- the aggregate ASC 310-10 impairment amount is included in the total ALLL, which includes loans that are impaired with an impairment amount of zero.

4. Assess whether the bank established its allowance for retail loans not evaluated individually for impairment consistent with the standards in ASC 450-20, "Loss Contingencies." Consider whether

- a robust credit risk grading (or segmentation) system forms the foundation for determining inherent loss.
- exposures are stratified into pools with similar risk characteristics including risk rating, line of business, industry, and product.
- documentation of the look-back period, the loss emergence period, loss factors, and other assumptions provide transparency and support that can be understood by an informed third party.
- judgmental factors (imprecision, qualitative factors, etc.) are quantified and well supported by a comprehensive analysis and narrative.
- use of economic data is well supported.
- reporting for both the board (or designated committee) and senior management provides sufficient detail to support the appropriateness of the ALLL balance at each quarter-end. Reports include details on ASC 310-10 impaired loans,[95] estimates of credit losses for ASC 450-20 pools of loans,[96] purchased credit impaired reserves, and management's documented rationale.

Personnel

Personnel are the bank staff and managers who execute or oversee processes. Personnel should be qualified and competent, have clearly defined responsibilities, and be held accountable for their actions. They should understand the bank's mission, risk appetite, core values, policies, and processes. Banks should design compensation programs to attract and retain personnel, align with strategy, and appropriately balance risk taking and reward.

Objective: Determine whether management expertise and staffing resources are appropriate for the volume, risk profile, and complexity of the products and services offered.

1. Using the organizational chart, discuss with senior management the backgrounds, responsibilities, and qualifications of key business and risk managers.

- Review and document the retail organizational structure and note any significant changes in senior management or staffing levels. Consider turnover trends for significant functional areas.
- Obtain criteria for key management compensation programs and position evaluations. Determine whether goals and objectives are consistent with the bank's risk appetite and business plan.

---

[95] A loan is impaired when, based on current information and events, it is probable that a creditor will be unable to collect all amounts due according to the contractual terms of the loan agreement.

[96] An example is homogeneous pools of non-impaired loans.

- Determine whether performance criteria include objective measures such as policy overrides, credit performance, and profitability for the retail portfolio as a whole, and segmented by significant product.
- Review key managers' performance-based compensation for the most recent evaluation period and assess whether managers are, in fact, held accountable for meeting agreed-upon objectives.

2. Obtain and review results of any resource or skill-gap assessments produced for business line managers or risk management functions. Consider whether

- gaps and assessment analyses consider current and planned activities.
- adequacy assessments include depth of staff succession planning for key positions.
- managers were required to respond in writing to identified gaps.
- identified gaps have either been addressed, or corrective plans are in place.

3. Assess whether staffing for the business line units (credit approval, loan originations, credit administration, collections, and portfolio management) are appropriate for the size, complexity, and risk profile of the bank. Consider the products offered, current and expected target markets, and actual and expected transaction volumes. Determine whether

- management experience and expertise align with the sophistication and complexity of the products offered and planned.
- staffing plans are consistent with department and bank objectives (e.g., growth and credit performance projections).
- staffing levels are sufficient for the scope of operations, complexity of the products, and volume of transactions expected.
- staff training in each area
  - is appropriate for the specific tasks assigned.
  - keeps pace with the complexity of the products, target markets, and transactions offered.
  - includes discussion of the bank's established risk appetite for retail lending.
- the board or senior management reviewed and approved all incentive pay programs before implementation.
- incentive pay programs
  - are consistent with the bank's business strategies and desired risk profile.
  - do not encourage volume over long-term credit quality, or shortcuts in due diligence or documentation due to time pressures.
  - appropriately limit the total incentive pay a loan originator or underwriter can receive.

4. Assess the structure, management, and staffing of each significant control function, including risk management, loan review, model risk governance, internal and external audit, quality assurance, and compliance review. Consider the retail lending products

offered, current and expected target markets, and actual and expected transaction volumes. Determine whether

- the roles, responsibilities, and reporting lines for each control function are appropriate, documented, and well communicated.
- staff expertise aligns with the sophistication and complexity of the products and services offered.
- the quality and depth of staff (including expertise and number) are adequate for the responsibilities assigned. Consider
  - the experience levels of managers and staff in control function roles.
  - the expertise of staff and managers with the products, transactions, or activities within their area of responsibility.
  - management and staff turnover levels.
- plans exist to address any known or anticipated gaps or vacancies.
- compensation plans and performance measurements are appropriately targeted to risk identification and control objectives.
- organizational reporting lines create the necessary level of independence.

Control Systems

Control systems are the functions (such as internal and external audit, and quality assurance) and information systems that bank managers use to measure performance, make decisions about risk, and assess the effectiveness of processes and personnel. Control functions should have clear reporting lines, sufficient resources, and appropriate access and authority. MIS should provide timely, accurate, and reliable information.

Objective: Assess the effectiveness of independent control function oversight of retail credit activities (e.g., risk management, loan review, model risk governance,[97] internal and external audit, quality assurance, and compliance review).[98]

1. Review the retail credit organizational chart to assess whether all retail credit activities are subject to review by qualified, independent control functions. Consider whether

- all significant products, services, and activities are subject to periodic independent control function review.
- organizational reporting lines establish the necessary level of independence.
- control function resources are sufficient to support assigned responsibilities, including the allocation and adequacy of staffing budgets.

---

[97] For more information, refer to OCC Bulletins 1997-24, "Credit Scoring Models: Examination Guidance," and 2011-12, "Sound Practices for Model Risk Management: Supervisory Guidance on Model Risk Management." Also refer to appendix F, "Credit Risk Model Oversight and Review Checklist," of this booklet.

[98] Compliance is a significant risk for retail lending. While consumer compliance examination activities generally assess the quality of the compliance review function, when assessing safety and soundness, examiners should understand compliance-related roles, responsibilities, and coverage, as well as how compliance controls fit into the overall control plan.

- current control function staffing levels appear sufficient for the scope and breadth of responsibilities.
- known or anticipated staffing gaps or vacancies have been adequately considered and addressed.

2. Evaluate independent control function management and staffing expertise. Consider whether

- control function managers have the business experience and product expertise to credibly opine on retail credit issues.
- control function staff has experience and expertise with the specific products and services offered.
- staff depth enables succession and continuation of coverage during times of change or adversity.
- continuing education and professional affiliation memberships are important.

3. Evaluate whether independent control functions have sufficient authority and standing to influence corrective action and curb inappropriate practices. Consider whether

- the audit committee (or board) actively sets expectations, approves policies and operating plans, and evaluates performance for each major independent control function.
- the audit committee (or board) approves the annual compensation and salary adjustment for each independent control function manager.
- the audit committee (or board) approves all decisions regarding the appointment or removal of independent control function managers.
- control function roles are defined and integrated into all significant risk management processes, including policy development, business strategy development, operations, information technology, and new product and service deployment.
- business line and operational departments openly expect and accept reviews and credible challenge exercises.
- the control function manager makes the final decisions on review conclusions, including program or initiative risk levels.
- significant issues require written management responses.
- management consistently responds to control system reviews in a timely manner with appropriate corrective action.
- issues identified and the status of corrective actions are tracked and reported to senior management or the board (or audit committee).
- control system managers have direct and unimpeded access to senior management and the board (or audit committee) and key risk issues are escalated in a timely manner.

4. Determine whether independent control functions have full control over the frequency, timing, and scope of reviews.[99] Consider whether

- rank ordering and scheduling of review areas come from the control function's own risk assessments and analysis.
- review cycles are consistent with risk assessments, and are reviewed and approved by the audit committee (or board) as part of its normal oversight responsibilities.
- review frequency is consistent with the significance of the risks involved.
- risk evaluations for significant new products or initiatives are a priority, and are completed in a timely manner.
- the scope of reviews includes transaction sample sizes sufficient to draw valid and supportable conclusions.
- the OCC and board can rely on the work and conclusions.

5. Review the normal scope of operations for independent risk management. Consider whether the function (or process)

- determines whether credit policies and procedures are appropriate for the portfolio's size, nature, complexity, and desired risk profile.
- monitors the risk profile in relation to the risk appetite.
- identifies systemic and emerging issues for retail credit overall, and for specific products and target markets.
- provides ongoing communication to the business lines regarding adherence to risk and concentration limits.
- escalates issues and concerns to appropriate parties or committees in a timely and effective manner.
- has an explicit responsibility to evaluate and monitor issues related to policy exceptions and concentration limits.
- evaluates whether internal controls are sufficient and operating effectively for the type and level of risks assumed by the bank.
- identifies best or leading practices and ensures these are replicated where appropriate.

6. Determine whether the scope of operations for each control function considers the adequacy of policies, procedures, and processes, as well as adherence to established guidelines. Consider whether coverage includes

- an assessment of the existing risk profile.
- the adequacy of policies and procedures to support decision-making and produce the intended levels of portfolio risk and performance.
- adherence to existing policies, procedures, and process maps.
- compliance with applicable laws and regulations, such as the BSA and consumer protection rules and consistency with guidance, including an assessment of whether any practices are discriminatory, unfair, deceptive, abusive, or predatory.

---

[99] Subject to audit committee approval of overall audit and control function plans.

- the identification, management, monitoring, and analysis of policy exceptions.
- the adequacy and reliability of management reporting.
- assessments of concentration levels and risk limits in the context of emerging risks and the established risk appetite.
- review of new underwriting.
- analysis and reporting on emerging trends.

7. Consider whether control function reports are issued in a timely manner and succinctly and clearly convey major findings. Determine whether reports consistently address

   - the adequacy of credit policies, procedures, process maps, information systems, and risk management controls.
   - adherence to established credit policies and procedures.
   - potential or emerging risks and concerns, including those involving strategic decisions or the easing of underwriting standards.
   - issues that span multiple lines of business.
   - the cause of identified problems.
   - objective measures to identify, measure, and monitor risk levels relative to prudent standards and established risk appetite.
   - the status of outstanding issues from previous reviews.

8. Assess whether transaction testing is a normal part of credit-related reviews. Consider whether samples effectively target

   - recently approved accounts, to assess adherence to credit approval policies.
   - recent exceptions to normal underwriting standards, to evaluate the adequacy and consistency of judgmental decisions.
   - loans that were 60 days or more delinquent two months ago and are now current, to evaluate cure and re-aging activities.
   - loans recently re-aged, extended, deferred, renewed, or re-written, for compliance with bank policy and reasonableness.
   - recently charged-off loans, to determine whether actions taken before the charge-off were reasonable or had the effect of deferring losses.
   - other samples to test for emerging issues, based on current economic or industry events.

Conclusions

Conclusion: The aggregate level of each associated risk is (low, moderate, or high). The direction of each associated risk is (increasing, stable, or decreasing).

Objective: Document and communicate findings and conclusions from the retail credit risk management examination.

1. Determine preliminary examination findings and conclusions and discuss with the examiner-in-charge, including

    - quantity of associated risks.
    - quality of risk management.
    - aggregate level and direction of associated risks.
    - overall risk in retail lending.
    - violations and other concerns.

Summary of Risks Associated With Retail Lending				
Risk category	Quantity of risk (Low, moderate, high)	Quality of risk management (Weak, insufficient, satisfactory, strong)	Aggregate level of risk (Low, moderate, high)	Direction of risk (Increasing, stable, decreasing)
Credit				
Interest rate				
Operational				
Liquidity				
Compliance				
Strategic				
Reputation				

2. If substantive safety and soundness concerns remain unresolved that may have a material adverse effect on the bank, further expand the scope of the examination by completing verification procedures.

3. Discuss examination findings with bank management, including violations, concerns, recommendations, and conclusions about risks and risk management practices. If necessary, obtain commitments for corrective action.

4. Compose conclusion comments, highlighting any issues that should be included in the report of examination. If necessary, compose a matters requiring attention comment.

5. Update the OCC's information system and any applicable report of examination schedules or tables.

6. Document findings from credit underwriting assessment in supervisory information system(s). If applicable, document findings and update the credit underwriting assessment system in the appropriate credit underwriting assessment module in Examiner View.

7. Update, organize, and reference work papers in accordance with OCC policy.

8. Ensure that any paper or electronic media that contain sensitive bank or customer information are appropriately disposed of or secured in accordance with OCC policy.

9. Write a memorandum or update the strategy specifically setting out what the OCC should do in the future to effectively supervise retail credit risk management in the bank, including time periods, staffing, and work days required.

Internal Control Questionnaire

An internal control questionnaire (ICQ) helps an examiner assess a bank's internal controls for an area. ICQs typically address standard controls that provide day-to-day protection of bank assets and financial records. The examiner decides the extent to which it is necessary to complete or update ICQs during examination planning or after reviewing the findings and conclusions of the core assessment.

1. Has the board, consistent with its duties and responsibilities, adopted written retail lending policies and objectives that establish

   - an outline of retail loan portfolio management objectives?
   - a definition of acceptable types of loans?
   - portfolio composition guidelines?
   - guidelines for aggregate outstanding loans and unfunded commitments in relation to other balance sheet categories?
   - the need to employ personnel with specialized knowledge and experience?
   - lending authority limits for committees and individual lending officers?
   - a definition of the duties and responsibilities of loan officers and loan committees?
   - maximum maturities for various types of loans?
   - loan pricing standards, guidelines, or processes?
   - appraisal and collateral valuation policies?
   - minimum financial information required at inception of credit?
   - limits and guidelines for purchasing loans from brokers, dealers, correspondents, and other third parties?
   - guidelines for loans to bank directors, officers, principal shareholders, and their related interests?
   - procedures for identifying and appropriately handling potential conflicts of interest.
   - collections procedures?
   - guidelines for compliance with applicable laws and regulations?

2. Are retail loan portfolio management policies and objectives reviewed at least annually to determine if they are compatible with changing market conditions?

3. Are the following reported to the board or its committees (indicate which) at their regular meetings:

   - Past-due single payment notes (if so, indicate the minimum days past due for them to be included)?
   - Notes on which interest-only is past due (if so, indicate the minimum days past due for them to be included)?
   - Term loans on which one installment is past due (if so, indicate the minimum days past due for them to be included)?
   - Outstanding balances under canceled advance (overdraft) facilities that are unpaid (if so, indicate the minimum days past due for them to be included)?

- Total outstanding loan commitments?
- Loans in workout, forbearance, or other programs requiring special attention?
- New loans and loan renewals or restructured loans?

4. Are reports submitted to the board or its committees rechecked by a designated individual for possible omissions before their submission?

5. Are written applications required for all loan types offered by the bank?

6. Does the bank maintain credit records for all borrowers?

7. Are loan records retained in accordance with record retention policy and legal requirements?

8. Does the credit documentation contain information on the

- purpose of the loan?
- planned repayment schedule?
- disposition of loan proceeds?

9. Does the bank perform a credit investigation on proposed and existing borrowers for new loan applications?

10. Are lines of credit reviewed and updated at least annually?

11. Are borrowers' outstanding liabilities checked to appropriate lines of credit before granting additional advances?

12. Does the bank employ a procedure for disclosure of a loan or combination of loans that are or will be secured by 25 percent of another insured financial institution's stock?

13. Is there an internal review system (it may be a function of the internal audit department) that covers each department and

- rechecks interest, discount, and maturity date computations?
- re-examines notes for proper execution, receipt of all required supporting papers, and proper disclosure forms?
- determines that loan approvals are within the limits of the bank's lending authorities?
- rechecks liability ledger to determine that new loans have been accurately posted?
- rechecks the preparation of maturity and interest notices?
- examines entries to various general ledger loan controls?
- confirms collateral, loans, and discounts with customers on a test basis?

14. Does the bank have a retail loan review function or the equivalent?

15. Is the retail loan review function independent of the lending function?

16. Are the results of the retail loan review process submitted to a person or committee who is also independent of the lending function?

17. Are all loans exceeding a certain dollar amount selected for review by loan review?

18. Are internal audits conducted at least annually for all lending areas?

19. Are follow-up procedures in effect for internally classified loans, including an update memorandum to the appropriate credit file or system notes?

20. Is a systematic and progressively stronger follow-up notice procedure utilized for delinquent loans?

21. Are paid and renewed notes cancelled and promptly returned to customers?

22. Do loan proceeds disbursed in cash require a customer receipt?

23. Does the bank maintain loan interest rate schedules for various types of loans?

24. Does the bank periodically update interest rate schedules (if so, state normal frequency)?

25. Does the bank maintain records in sufficient detail to generate the following information by type of advance:

    - Cost of funds loaned?
    - Cost of servicing loans, including overhead?
    - Cost factor of probable losses?
    - Programmed profit margin?

26. Has the bank conducted industry studies for those industries in which it is a substantial lender?

Conclusion

27. Is the foregoing information considered an adequate basis for evaluating internal control in that there are no significant additional internal auditing procedures, accounting controls, administrative controls, or other circumstances that impair any controls or mitigate any weaknesses indicated in this ICQ (explain negative answers briefly, and indicate conclusions as to their effect on specific examination or verification procedures)?

28. Based on a composite evaluation as evidenced by answers to the foregoing questions, internal control is considered (strong, satisfactory, insufficient, or weak).

Verification Procedures

Verification procedures are used to verify the existence of assets and liabilities, or test the reliability of financial records. Examiners generally do not perform verification procedures as part of a typical examination. Rather, verification procedures are performed when substantive safety and soundness concerns are identified that are not mitigated by the bank's risk management practices and internal controls.

Objective: Verify the authenticity of the bank's retail loans, and test the accuracy of records and adequacy of record keeping.

Note: Examiners normally do not have to do extensive verification. These procedures are appropriate, however, when the bank has inadequate audit coverage of retail lending activities or when fraud or other irregularities are suspected.

1. Test the additions of the trial balances and the reconciliation of the trial balances to the general ledger. Include loan commitments and other contingent liabilities.

2. After selecting loans from the trial balance by using an appropriate sampling technique,

   - prepare and mail confirmation forms to borrowers. (Loans serviced by other institutions, either whole loans or participations, are usually confirmed only with the servicing institution. Loans serviced for other institutions, either whole loans or participations, should be confirmed with the buying institution and the borrower. Confirmation forms should include borrower's name, loan number, the original loan amount, interest rate, current loan balance, borrowing base, and a brief description of the collateral).[100]
   - after a reasonable time, mail second requests.
   - follow up on any unanswered requests for verification or exceptions and resolve differences.
   - examine notes for completeness and compare agreement date, amount, and terms with trial balance.
   - in the event notes are not held at the bank, request confirmation by the holder.
   - confirm that required officer approvals are on the note.
   - confirm that note is signed, appears to be genuine, and is negotiable.
   - if the loan is secured,
     - determine whether the proper collateral documentation is on file.
     - compare collateral held in loan files with the description on the loan documents.
     - determine whether advance rates and LTV ratios are reasonable and in line with bank policy.
     - list and investigate all collateral discrepancies.

---

[100] Direct confirmation with bank customers must have prior approval of the Assistant Deputy Comptroller and district Deputy Comptroller or appropriate large bank supervisors. See the "Internal and External Audits" booklet of the *Comptroller's Handbook.*

    − determine that any required insurance coverage is adequate and that the bank is named as loss payee.

3. Review disbursement ledgers and authorizations, and determine whether authorizations are signed in accordance with the terms of the loan agreement.

4. Review accounts with accrued interest by

   - reviewing and testing procedures for accounting for accrued interest and for handling adjustments.
   - scanning accrued interest for any unusual entries and following up on any unusual items by tracing them to initial and supporting records.

5. Using a list of nonaccrual loans, check loan accrual records to determine that interest income is not being recorded.

6. Obtain or prepare a schedule showing the monthly interest income amounts and the retail loan balance at each month-end since the last examination, and

   - calculate yield.
   - investigate any significant fluctuations or trends.

Appendixes

Appendix A: Sample Request Letter

Examiners should tailor the following request letter as needed, based on the scope of the examination and the nature of the bank's activities.

Please provide the following information for retail lending activities as of the close of business on (DATE), unless otherwise indicated. Information in an electronic format is preferred. If submitting hard copies, please prominently mark any information or documentation that is to be returned to the bank.

The OCC's intent is to request information that can be easily obtained. If you find that the information is not readily available or requires significant effort on your part to prepare, please contact us before compiling the data.

Please note that this list is not all-inclusive and that we may request additional items during the course of our examination.

General

1. Organizational chart(s) for the retail lending organization, including its key executives and risk managers. For key executives and risk managers, please include a brief summary of their job description, background, qualifications, and experience levels in relation to their current responsibilities.

2. A list of primary contacts, including contact numbers.

3. A list of board and formal management committees that provide credit-related oversight. For each, please provide

   a. a list of members and meeting schedules.
   b. meeting minutes for the most recent full year and year to date.
   c. a copy of the standard report package distributed at, or in advance of, each meeting.
   d. committee charter.

4. Copies of strategic, business, and operating plans for retail lending overall, and for each significant retail product. Include projections, budgets, assumptions, and supporting details used to prepare or communicate the plan(s).

5. Copies of risk appetite statements developed for the bank as a whole, for retail lending overall, and for any developed for significant retail lending products.

6. Copies of risk assessment evaluations performed for retail lending as a whole, and for any significant retail lending products or portfolios.

7. A high-level summary of the bank's retail credit business. For each retail credit product offered, please provide

   a. a brief description of the product, including its basic characteristics and terms.
   b. summary tables of the dollars outstanding, number of accounts, and volume of unfunded commitments. Please include the current quarter and the eight quarters prior.
   c. descriptions of marketing or acquisition channels used (e.g., direct, Internet, mail, and third-party originators).
   d. descriptions of any new or expanded features, market segments, or marketing initiatives since the last examination or planned for the near future. Please include any written product proposals and projections for new, modified, or expanded products introduced within the last 18 months.
   e. written analyses or proposals for any retail product or product segment discontinued or significantly curtailed within the last 18 months.
   f. descriptions of any third-party loan origination, account management, collections, or other account service arrangements in place.
   g. descriptions of all credit models or scorecards used in credit originations, account management, collections, or portfolio management.
   h. descriptions of any portfolios acquired since the last examination, including due diligence reports.
   i. a brief summary and description of any securitization, loan purchases or sales, credit derivatives, or other concentration or liquidity management activities related to retail lending products or portfolios.

8. A brief description of litigation, either filed or anticipated, associated with the bank's retail lending activities. Include expected costs or other implications.

9. Customer complaint logs for retail loans since the last examination.

Credit Risk Management Framework

10. A written description of the risk management framework for retail lending activities. Please describe the processes in place for

    a. performing periodic risk assessments for retail lending overall, and for each significant retail product.
    b. establishing a risk appetite statement for retail lending overall, and for each significant retail product (if applicable).
    c. establishing business plans and operating strategies for retail lending overall, and for each significant retail product.
    d. establishing concentration, risk, and other borrower or portfolio limits at the retail credit and significant retail product levels.

11. For each process described in procedure 10 a-d above, please identify

    e. the specific policy or operating procedure that governs the activity.
    f. responsible parties and key contacts.
    g. the timing and schedule for development, updates, or modifications.
    h. reports, studies, or presentations used to discuss and monitor related activity by the board, senior management, or other oversight committees.
    i. the most recent independent control function review (internal audit, external audit, risk management, etc.) for each, including management's response to any issues or deficiencies.

12. Description of controls (e.g., financial and audit requirements) and performance reports used to monitor third parties' quality of service, as well as due diligence criteria used to select third parties for the retail activities.

Credit Originations

13. A complete process flow chart and description of the account screening, underwriting, and verification processes for a new account. If processes vary by product, include each. The process flow diagram and description should clearly note functions and identities of activities performed by third parties.

14. A complete process flow chart and description for modifying, renewing, or refinancing existing loans.

15. Copies of loan policies and operating procedures for each retail product offered.

16. An inventory and description of all management reports produced regularly to supervise retail credit originations. For each major report, please describe the distribution list, the frequency of distribution, and the person or unit responsible for preparation.

17. A description of the process used to identify, manage, and monitor exceptions to credit origination-related policies and operating procedures. Please include copies of reports used to monitor policy exceptions and overrides. Include any analyses of subsequent performance by type of exception.

18. Risk management reports used to monitor and analyze applicant quality and trends. Include application-tracking trend reports for the most recent year-end and year to date. Depending on the portfolio, information may include applications submitted, approved, booked, and denied; underwriting criteria, such as credit grades, loan-to-value ratios, credit scores, and debt-to-income distributions or measures; and credit scorecard monitoring reports, such as Kolmogorov-Smirnov tests, population stability, and characteristic analysis.

19. Reports used to track loan officer or underwriter productivity and compliance with policy.

20. If dealers, brokers, or other third-party originators are used, copies of the management reports used to monitor the quality of applicants and credit performance of loans sourced from each third party used.

21. If debt suspension, debt cancellation or other add-on products are offered, please provide management reports used to monitor product performance. Include information for product penetration, claims rates (approved and denied), reserve method and balances, and profitability.

Credit Administration and Collections

22. A complete process flow chart for post-approval account processing. As applicable, include flow charts for authorizations, balance control, retention, cross-selling, collections, fraud control, and any other significant account administration process.

23. An inventory and description of all management reports produced regularly to supervise credit administration and collections. For each major report, please describe the distribution list, the frequency of distribution, and the person or unit responsible for preparation.

24. A description and example of ad hoc reports produced over the last 18 months to consider or manage any significant credit administration or collections issue.

25. A description of how the bank segments retail portfolios for credit quality and portfolio composition monitoring purposes. If segmentation differs by product or portfolio, describe each significant approach.

26. An overview of how the bank's credit administration and collections operations conform to OCC Bulletin 2000-20, "Uniform Retail Credit Classification and Account Management Policy: Policy Implementation."

27. Summary reports for the volume and trends for loan extensions, including subsequent performance monitoring.

28. Summary reports for the volume and trends of accounts in workout programs (e.g., Consumer Credit Counseling Service) or other forbearance programs, including subsequent performance monitoring.

29. Summary reports used to monitor the volume and trends for repossessed collateral, as well as remarketing efforts. Include inventory aging and monthly trends for units, dollars, and deficiency loss trends.

30. Copies of management reports used to manage and measure the effectiveness of the collection area (e.g., roll-rates, dollars collected, and promises to pay).

31. Copies of management reports detailing the number and dollar amounts of first payment defaults. If available, include monthly reports for the last 12 months.

32. Reports used to monitor collections, loss mitigation, or workout program policy exceptions and overrides. Include any analyses of subsequent performance by type of exception.

33. A description of credit quality or volume triggers or guardrails used to note potential problems or issues. Include triggers for consumer lending overall, and those applicable to specific products or portfolios.

34. A description of the results of the most recent stress tests for retail lending as a whole and for each significant product or portfolio. Include methodologies, and any written presentations or analysis of results and follow-up actions.

Control Functions

35. An organizational chart and brief description of each retail-credit-related control function (risk management, internal audit, loan review, quality control and quality assurance, third-party relationship risk management, model risk management, etc.).

36. A schedule of all control function reviews performed within the last 18 months. Include scope summaries for each review.

37. Examples of open-item monitoring reports for each control function. Include production frequency and distribution lists for each report.

ALLL

38. Most recent allowance for loan and lease losses analysis for the retail portfolio overall, and for each significant product or portfolio. Include a complete description of the method and assumptions used.

Appendix B: Quantity of Retail Credit Risk Indicators

Estimating the quantity of retail credit risk is an important element in the evaluation of retail credit risk management. The OCC expects risk management activities to be commensurate with the size, complexity, and risk profile of the bank. To determine the quantity of retail credit risk, examiners should consider an array of quantitative and qualitative risk measurements. These indicators can be leading (rapid growth), lagging (high past-due levels), static (point in time evaluation/gauge), relative (exceeds peer/historical norms), or dynamic (trend or change in portfolio mix). Many of these indicators are readily available from internal MIS as well as call report and Uniform Bank Performance Report information. Other indicators, such as the bank's risk appetite or underwriting practices, while more subjective, should also be considered. Examiners may use the following indicators to supplement their analysis of the quantity of credit risk.

Low	Moderate	High
The level of loans outstanding is low relative to total assets and equity capital.	The level of loans outstanding is moderate relative to total assets and equity capital.	The level of loans outstanding is high relative to total assets and equity capital.
Growth rates are supported by local, regional, or national economic and demographic trends and level of competition. Growth (including off-balance-sheet activities) has been planned for and appears consistent with management and staff expertise or operational capabilities.	Growth rates exceed local, regional, or national economic and demographic trends and level of competition. Some growth (including off-balance-sheet activities) has not been planned or exceeds planned levels and may test management and staff expertise or operational capabilities.	Growth rates significantly exceed local, regional, or national economic and demographic trends and level of competition. Growth (including off-balance-sheet activities) was not planned or exceeds planned levels, and stretches management and staff expertise or operational capabilities. Growth may be in new products or with out-of-area borrowers.
The bank has well-diversified income, and dependence on interest and fees from loans and leases is commensurate with asset mix. Loan yields are low and risks/returns are well balanced.	The bank is dependent on interest and fees from loans for the majority of its income, but income sources within the loan portfolio are diversified. Loan yields are moderate. Imbalances between risk and return may exist but are not significant.	The bank is highly dependent on interest and fees from loans and leases. It may target higher-risk loan products for their earnings potential. Loan income is highly vulnerable to cyclical trends. Loan yields are high and reflect an imbalance between risk and return, or risk is disproportionately high relative to return.
The bank's portfolio is well diversified with no single large concentrations or a few moderate concentrations. Concentrations are well within internal limits. Change in portfolio mix is neutral or reduces overall risk profile.	The bank has one or two material concentrations. Concentrations are in compliance with internal guidelines but may be approaching the limits. Change in portfolio mix may increase overall risk profile.	The bank has one or more large concentrations. Concentrations may have exceeded internal limits. Change in portfolio mix significantly increases overall risk profile.

Low	Moderate	High
Existing or new extensions of credit reflect conservative underwriting and risk-selection standards. Policies are conservative and exceptions are nominal.	Existing or new extensions of credit generally reflect conservative to moderate underwriting and risk-selection standards. Policies and exceptions are moderate.	Existing or new extensions of credit reflect liberal underwriting and risk-selection standards. Policies either allow such practices or practices have resulted in a large number of exceptions.
Underwriting policies are reasonable. Underwriting standards for loans held for sale or originated to distribute are reasonable and consistent with standards for loans made with the intention of being held for the bank's portfolio. The bank has only occasional loans with structural weaknesses or underwriting exceptions. Those loans are well mitigated and do not constitute an undue risk.	Underwriting policies are satisfactory. Underwriting standards for loans held for sale or originated to distribute are reasonable but are inconsistent with loans made with the intention of being held for the bank's portfolio. The bank has an average level of loans with structural weaknesses or exceptions to sound underwriting standards consistent with balancing competitive pressures and reasonable growth objectives.	Underwriting policies are inadequate. Underwriting standards for loans held for sale or originated to distribute are inconsistent with loans made with the intention of being held for the bank's portfolio. The bank has a high level of loans with structural weaknesses or underwriting exceptions that expose the bank to heightened loss in the event of default.
Collateral requirements are conservative. Collateral valuations are timely and well supported.	Collateral requirements are acceptable. Bank practices result in moderate deviations from policy. A moderate number of collateral valuations are not well supported or reflect inadequate protection. Soft (intangible) collateral is sometimes used in lieu of hard (tangible) collateral.	Collateral requirements are liberal, or if policies incorporate conservative requirements, there are substantial deviations. Collateral valuations are not always obtained, frequently unsupported or reflect inadequate protection. Soft (intangible) collateral is frequently used rather than hard (tangible) collateral.
Loan documentation or collateral exceptions are low and have minimal impact on risk of loss.	The level of loan documentation or collateral exceptions is moderate, but exceptions are corrected in a timely manner and generally do not expose the bank to risk of loss.	The level of loan documentation or collateral exceptions is high. Exceptions are outstanding for inordinate periods and the bank may be exposed to heightened risk of loss.
Distribution across pass categories is consistent with a conservative risk appetite. Migration trends within the pass category are balanced or favor the higher or less risky ratings. Lagging indicators, such as past dues and nonaccruals, are low and the trend is stable.	Distribution across pass categories is consistent with a moderate risk appetite. Migration trends within the pass category are starting to favor the lower or riskier pass ratings. Lagging indicators, such as past dues and nonaccruals, are moderate and the trend is stable or rising slightly.	Distribution across pass categories is heavily skewed toward the lower or riskier pass ratings. Downgrades dominate rating changes within the pass category. Lagging indicators, such as past dues and nonaccruals, are moderate or high and the trend is rising.
Classified and special-mention loans represent a low percentage of loans and capital and are not skewed to the more severe categories (doubtful or loss).	Classified and special-mention loans represent a moderate percentage of loans and capital and are not skewed to the more severe categories (doubtful or loss).	Classified and special-mention loans represent a high percentage of loans and capital, or a moderate percentage of loans and capital and are growing, or are skewed to the more severe categories (doubtful or loss).

Low	Moderate	High
Bank re-aging, extension, renewal, and refinancing practices raise little or no concern about the accuracy/transparency of reported problem loan, past due, nonperforming, and loss numbers.	Bank re-aging, extension, renewal, and refinancing practices raise some concern about the accuracy/transparency of reported problem loan, past due, nonperforming, and loss numbers.	Bank re-aging, extension, renewal, and refinancing practices raise substantial concern about the accuracy/transparency of reported problem loan, past due, nonperforming, and loss numbers.
Loan losses to total loans are low. ALLL coverage of problem and noncurrent loans and loan losses is high. Provision expense is stable.	Loan losses to total loans are moderate. ALLL coverage of problem and noncurrent loans is moderate, but provision expense may need to be increased.	Loan losses to total loans are high. ALLL coverage of problem and noncurrent loans is low. Special provisions may be needed to maintain acceptable coverage.

Appendix C: Quality of Credit Risk Management Indicators

Examiners may use the following indicators to supplement their assessment of the quality of credit risk management. (For comprehensive guidelines on portfolio management, refer to the "Loan Portfolio Management" booklet of the *Comptroller's Handbook*.)

Strong	Satisfactory	Insufficient	Weak
There is a clear, sound credit culture. Board and senior management's risk appetite is well communicated and understood.	The credit culture is generally sound, but may vary by product line or business unit. Risk appetite may not be clearly communicated throughout the bank.	Credit culture may not be well understood. Risk appetite may be inconsistent with strategic goals or not uniformly communicated throughout the bank.	Credit culture is absent or is materially flawed. Risk appetite may not be well understood or is ineffective in controlling aggregate or key portfolio risks.
Strategic or business plans are consistent with risk appetite and promote an appropriate balance between risk taking and growth and earnings objectives. New loan products/initiatives are well researched, tested, and approved before implementation.	Strategic or business plans are consistent with risk appetite. Anxiety for income may lead to some higher-risk transactions. Generally, an appropriate balance exists between risk taking and growth and earnings objectives. New loan products/initiatives may be launched with some limited testing and risk analysis. This analysis is likely not robust but is sufficient to quantify the potential risk.	Strategic or business plans are not fully consistent with risk appetite. Anxiety for income may lead to some higher-risk transactions that may not be well understood. There is an imbalance between risk taking and growth and earnings objectives. New loan products/initiatives may be launched without sufficient testing and risk analysis.	Strategic or business plans are inconsistent with risk appetite or may encourage taking on excessive levels of risk. Anxiety for income dominates planning activities. The bank engages in new loan products/initiatives without conducting sufficient due diligence testing.
Management is effective. Loan management and personnel possess extensive expertise to effectively administer the risk assumed. Responsibilities and accountability are clear, and appropriate and timely remedial or corrective action is taken when they are breached.	Management is adequate to administer assumed risk, but improvements may be needed in one or more areas. Loan management and personnel generally possess the expertise required to effectively administer assumed risks, but additional expertise may be required in one or more areas. Responsibilities and accountability may require some clarification. Generally, appropriate remedial or corrective action is taken to address the root causes of problems.	Management requires improvement and strengthening in one or more key areas. Responsibilities and accountability likely require some clarification or do not reflect the bank's current structure. Management may take remedial or corrective actions to address root causes of problems, but these actions are not always effective or timely.	Management is deficient. Loan management and personnel may not possess sufficient expertise or experience, or otherwise may demonstrate an unwillingness to effectively administer the risk assumed. Responsibilities and accountability are not clear. Remedial or corrective actions are lacking or do not address root causes of problems.

Strong	Satisfactory	Insufficient	Weak
Diversification strategies are active and effective. Concentration limits are set at reasonable levels. The bank identifies and reports concentrated exposures and initiates actions to limit, reduce, or otherwise mitigate risk. Management identifies and understands correlated exposure risks.	Diversification strategies are adequate. Concentrated exposures are identified and reported. Management has set reasonable concentration limits, but these limits may require minor enhancements or further stratification. Management generally takes action to limit, reduce, or otherwise mitigate risk. Correlated exposures are understood but may not be formally discussed or well documented.	Diversification strategies need improvement. Management has set concentration limits, but these limits may not be reasonable, are outdated, or may not adequately address the primary exposures at the bank. Management may identify when the bank exceeds these limits but does not always take appropriate or timely actions to reduce or mitigate risk when limits are exceeded. Correlated exposures are not well understood or clearly identified.	Diversification strategies are deficient or altogether absent. The bank takes little or no action to limit, reduce, or mitigate risk. Management does not understand exposure correlations. Concentration limits, if any, may be exceeded or are raised frequently.
Loan management and personnel compensation structures provide appropriate balance between loan/revenue production, loan quality, and portfolio administration, including risk identification.	Loan management and personnel compensation structures provide reasonable balance between loan/revenue production, loan quality, and portfolio administration.	Loan management and personnel compensation structures may be skewed toward loan/revenue production. There may be inadequate incentives or accountability for loan quality and portfolio administration.	Loan management and personnel compensation structures are skewed to loan/revenue production. There is little evidence of substantive incentives or accountability for loan quality and portfolio administration.
Staffing levels and expertise are robust for the size and complexity of the loan portfolio. Staff turnover is reasonable and allows for the orderly transfer of responsibilities. Training programs facilitate ongoing staff development.	Staffing levels and expertise are generally adequate for the size and complexity of the loan portfolio. Staff turnover is moderate, but management addresses gaps in portfolio management in a timely manner. Training initiatives are effective but may need minor enhancements.	Staffing levels need improvement. High turnover may result in significant gaps in some areas. Management and the board do not respond to these needs in a timely manner. Training initiatives may be present but are likely inconsistent.	Staffing levels are inadequate in numbers or skill level. Turnover is high and management and the board are ineffective at addressing staffing gaps or shortfalls. Training is lacking or wholly insufficient.
Lending policies effectively establish and communicate portfolio objectives, risk appetite, and underwriting and risk-selection standards.	Policies are fundamentally adequate. Enhancements can be achieved in one or more areas but are generally not critical. Specificity of risk appetite or underwriting and risk-selection standards may need improvement to fully communicate policy requirements.	Credit-related policies require improvement. They may not be sufficiently clear or are too general to adequately communicate portfolio objectives, risk appetite, and underwriting and risk-selection standards. Policies may be outdated or do not reflect the board's risk appetite.	Policies are deficient in one or more ways and require significant improvement in several areas. Key policies may be absent or lack basic credit guidance on risk appetite, underwriting criteria, or risk-selection standards.

Strong	Satisfactory	Insufficient	Weak
Bank effectively identifies, approves, tracks, and reports significant policy, underwriting, and risk-selection exceptions individually and in aggregate, including risk exposures associated with off-balance-sheet activities.	Bank identifies, approves, and reports significant policy, underwriting, and risk-selection exceptions on a loan-by-loan basis, including risk exposures associated with off-balance-sheet activities. Little aggregation or trend analysis is conducted to determine the effect on portfolio quality.	Bank approves significant policy exceptions but may not report them individually or in aggregate, or may not analyze their effect on portfolio quality. Risk exposures associated with off-balance-sheet activities may not be considered.	Bank does not have an effective process to identify or approve significant policy exceptions. Risk exposures associated with off-balance-sheet activities are not considered or understood.
Credit analysis is thorough and timely both at underwriting and periodically thereafter.	Credit analysis appropriately identifies key risks and is conducted within reasonable time frames. Analysis after underwriting is effective but may need minor enhancements.	Credit analysis needs improvement. Moderate errors may be evident, key risks may be overlooked, or analyses may not be consistently timely. Further employee training or assistance is required.	Credit analysis is deficient. Analysis is not timely, accurate, or complete and cannot be relied on for underwriting or risk rating decisions. Employees lack basic knowledge or understanding of how to complete these analyses.
Internal or outsourced risk rating and problem loan review/identification systems are accurate and timely. They effectively stratify credit risk in both problem and pass-rated credits. They serve as an effective early warning tool and support risk-based pricing, ALLL, and capital allocation processes.	Internal or outsourced risk rating and problem loan review/identification systems are effective in identifying problem and emerging problem credits. Examiners or loan review may have identified a small but explainable number of exceptions. The graduation of pass ratings may need to be expanded to facilitate early warning, risk-based pricing, or capital allocation.	Internal or outsourced risk rating and problem loan review/identification systems require improvement. Problem credits may be identified, but not in a timely manner, and exceptions are moderate to high. The graduation of pass ratings is insufficient to stratify risk in pass-rated credits for early warning or other purposes (loan pricing, ALLL, capital allocation).	Internal or outsourced risk rating and problem loan review/identification systems are deficient. The bank does not have an effective system to accurately or promptly identify problem credits; as a result, portfolio risk is significantly misstated.

Strong	Satisfactory	Insufficient	Weak
Loan review (either internal or external) is comprehensive, timely, and effective. Loan review identifies underwriting, financial, and collateral exceptions and also evaluates the adequacy of overall credit risk management. Management and personnel are qualified, experienced, and independent, and report directly to the board or its designated committee. Identified issues are resolved promptly and effectively. Work papers fully support conclusions.	Loan review (either internal or external) is adequate in scope, timely, and generally effective. Minor weaknesses may be evident. Loan review identifies underwriting, financial, and collateral exceptions but may not evaluate the overall credit risk management function. Management and personnel are qualified, experienced, and independent (whenever possible), and report directly to the board or its designated committee. Identified issues are generally resolved promptly and effectively. Work papers adequately support conclusions.	Loan review's (either internal or external) scope requires some expansion to ensure it is sufficient, or reviews may not always be timely. Reviews do not consistently identify underwriting, financial, and collateral exceptions and likely do not include an evaluation of overall credit risk management. Management or personnel may lack extensive experience, require further training, or may not be fully independent. Reporting to the board or a designated committee may be indirect. Work papers may not fully support all findings.	Loan review's (either internal or external) scope is inadequate and reviews are not timely, resulting in excessive lapses in coverage. The bank does not have a system to accurately identify underwriting, financial, or collateral exceptions. Management and personnel lack experience and competence, and independence may be in question. Key issues are not properly reported to the board or designated committee. Work papers are inadequate to support findings.
MIS provides accurate, timely, and complete portfolio information. Management and the board receive comprehensive reports to analyze and understand the bank's credit risk profile, including off-balance-sheet activities. MIS facilitates exception reporting, and MIS infrastructure can support ad hoc queries in a timely manner.	MIS may require minor improvement in one or more areas, but management and the board generally receive appropriate reports to analyze and understand the bank's credit risk profile. MIS facilitates exception reporting, and MIS infrastructure can support ad hoc queries in a timely manner.	MIS requires improvement. Reports may be incomplete or are not consistently produced in a timely fashion. As a result, management and the board may not be receiving complete information to fully analyze and understand the bank's credit risk profile. Exception reporting requires improvement, and MIS infrastructure may not support ad hoc queries in a timely manner.	MIS is deficient, lacks key information, is not timely, or is not reliable due to significant inaccuracies. As a result, management and the board are not receiving accurate or sufficient information to analyze and understand the bank's credit risk profile. The bank lacks exception reporting, and MIS infrastructure does not support ad hoc queries.

Appendix D: Uniform Retail Credit Classification and Account Management Policy Checklist
(RCCP Checklist)

Retail Credit Classification and Account Management Policy		
	Reference	Comments
Retail credit classification and account management policy (RCCP) applicability: • Closed-end credit extended to customers for household, family, and other personal expenditures. Includes consumer loans and credit cards. • Loans to customers secured by their personal residence, including first mortgage, home equity, and home improvement loans.		
Note regarding minimum policy guidelines • The RCCP does not preclude examiners from classifying individual loans or entire portfolios regardless of delinquency status or criticizing account management practices that are deficient or improperly managed. If underwriting, risk management, or account management standards are weak and present unreasonable credit risk, deviation from the minimum classification guidelines outlined in the policy may be prudent. • Credit losses should be recognized when the bank becomes aware of the loss, but should not exceed the time frames stated in the policy.		
	Reference	Comments
Substandard classification • Does the bank consider closed-end retail loans 90 cumulative days past due substandard? • When the bank does not hold the senior mortgage on a home equity loan, does it consider the loan substandard if it is 90 days or more past due, even if the LTV ratio is 60 percent or less (see note below)? • For loans to borrowers in bankruptcy, does the bank appropriately classify the loans as substandard until the borrower reestablishes the ability and willingness to repay for a period of at least six months, even when the bank can clearly demonstrate that repayment is likely to occur? **Note:** The policy states that properly secured residential real estate loans with LTV ratios of 60 percent or less may not need to be classified based solely on delinquency.		
Loss classification • Are unsecured closed-end retail loans charged off in the month they become 120 cumulative days past due? • Are secured closed-end retail loans secured by other than real estate collateral charged off in the month they become 120 cumulative days past due? – If not, are these loans written down to the value of the collateral, less cost to sell, **if** repossession of collateral is assured and in process? • For closed-end loans secured by residential real estate, is a current assessment of value made no later than when the account is 180 days past due? – For such loans, is any loan balance in excess of the value of the property, less cost to sell, charged off?		

Retail Credit Classification and Account Management Policy	Reference	Comments
Bankruptcy • Are loans in bankruptcy charged off within 60 days of receipt of notification of filing from the bankruptcy court unless the bank can document or support that repayment is likely to occur or within the 120- or 180-day time frame (whichever is shorter)? • Are loans with collateral written down to the value of collateral, less cost to sell? • When a loan's balance is not charged off, does the bank classify it as substandard until the borrower re-establishes the ability and willingness to repay for a period of at least six months?		
Fraudulent loans • Are fraudulent loans classified loss and charged off within 90 days of discovery or within the 120- or 180-day time frame (whichever is shorter)?		
Accounts of deceased persons • Are loans to deceased persons classified loss and charged off when the loss is determined or within the 120- or 180-day time frame (whichever is shorter)?		
Other considerations for classification • Under what conditions would the bank not classify (substandard or loss) a loan in accordance with the policy? **Note:** The policy permits non-classification if the bank can document that the loan is well secured and in the process of collection, such that collection will occur regardless of delinquency status.		
Partial payments • Does the bank require that a payment be equivalent to 90 percent or greater of the contractual payment before counting the payment as a full payment? • As an alternative, does the bank aggregate payments and give credit for any partial payments received? • Are controls in place to prevent both methods above from being used simultaneously on the same credit?		
Re-aging, extensions, deferrals, renewals, and rewrites • Are the above types of activities permitted only when the action is based on a renewed willingness and ability to repay the loan? • Does documentation show that the bank communicated with the borrower, the borrower agreed to pay the loan in full, and the borrower has the ability to repay the loan? • Do MIS separately identify the number of accounts and dollar amounts that have been re-aged, extended, deferred, renewed, or rewritten, including the number of times such actions have been taken? • How does the bank monitor and track the volume and performance of loans that have been re-aged, extended, deferred, renewed, rewritten, or placed in a workout program?		

Retail Credit Classification and Account Management Policy		
	Reference	Comments
Note: The issues above do not apply to customer-service-originated extensions or program extensions (such as holiday skip-a-pay). Examples of how the bank would determine and document the borrower's willingness and ability to repay could include such items as credit bureau score and data being obtained and reviewed, stated income being verified, and obtaining a "hardship" letter from the borrower.		

Closed-end credit (standards, controls, and MIS for each area)
 	
• Has the bank adopted and adhered to explicit standards that control the use of extensions, deferrals, renewals, and rewrites?
 	
• Do the standards include the following:
 	
  – Borrower has shown a renewed willingness and ability to repay the loan?
 	
  – Limits on the number and frequency of extensions, deferrals, renewals, and rewrites?
 	
• Are additional advances to finance unpaid interest and fees prohibited?
 	
• Do MIS track the subsequent principal reductions and charge-off history of loans that have been granted an extension, deferral, renewal, or rewrite?		

Appendix E: Account Management and Loss Allowance Checklist

Applicability: This checklist can be used to evaluate account management and loan-loss reserve practices for banks that offer open-end credit products (credit cards, HELOCs, check credit, etc.). Most of the line items pertain to credit card programs, but the concepts apply to all open-end credit, and can be used to evaluate general risk management practices. Examiners should consult applicable regulations, as appropriate, particularly those relating to closed-end loans.[101]

Note: Negative responses may indicate a higher level of risk that warrant stronger risk management practices. In such cases, further review may be necessary to determine appropriate practices to mitigate the risks.

Account Management and Loss Allowance Checklist			
	Yes/no	Doc. ref.	Comments
Credit line management 1. Does bank management test, analyze, and document line-assignment and line-increase criteria before broad implementation? 2. Does the bank offer customers multiple credit lines, such as bank card plus store-specific private-label cards and affinity relationship cards? If so, do the bank's MIS aggregate related exposures and does management analyze performance before offering additional credit lines? **Note:** Support for credit line management should include documentation and analysis of decision factors such as repayment history, risk scores, behavior scores, or other relevant criteria.			
Over-limit practices 1. Are policies and controls in place regarding over-limit authorizations? 2. Are fees or charges associated with an over-limit transaction assessed only after a borrower's consent or opt-in? 3. Does bank management take appropriate actions to facilitate the timely repayment of the over-limit amounts (e.g., reduce or eliminate fees, raise the minimum payment, initiate workout programs)?			

---

[101] For example, in connection with reviews of workout and forbearance, consider 12 CFR 1024.38 through 12 CFR 1024.41. In the context of closed-end loans, there are underwriting and ability-to-repay provisions that affect the ability to offer negative amortization loans. For example, refer to 12 CFR 1026.32, 1026.34, and 1026.43.

Account Management and Loss Allowance Checklist			
	Yes/no	Doc. ref.	Comments
4. Do MIS enable management to identify, measure, monitor, and control the unique risks associated with over-limit accounts? MIS should include the following: • Over-limit volume, segmented by severity. • Credit performance. • Duration of over-limit.			
Minimum payment and negative amortization 1. Do minimum payment requirements ensure that the principal balance will be amortized over a reasonable period of time, consistent with the risk profile of the borrower? 2. Do minimum payment requirements cover finance charges and recurring fees assessed during the billing cycle? **Note:** Liberal repayment programs can result in negative amortization (where outstanding balances continue to build). Prolonged negative amortization, inappropriate fees, and other practices can inordinately compound or protract consumer debt, mask portfolio performance and quality, and raise safety and soundness concerns. These practices should be criticized.			
Workout and forbearance practices **Note:** An open-end credit card account is a workout when its credit is no longer available and its balance owed is placed on a fixed (dollar or percentage) repayment schedule in accordance with modified, concessionary terms and conditions. Temporary hardship programs are not considered workout programs unless the program exceeds 12 months, including renewals. **Repayment period** 1. Do all workout programs provide for repayment terms that have borrowers repay their existing debt within 60 months? 2. What exceptions are allowed to the 60-month time frame? Are such exceptions clearly documented and supported by compelling evidence that less conservative terms and conditions are warranted? **Settlements** 3. For credit card accounts subject to settlement arrangements, are controls in place for setting the amount (dollar or percentage) to be forgiven and the requirement for the borrower to pay the remaining balance in either a lump-sum payment or in a period not to exceed three months?			

Account Management and Loss Allowance Checklist			
	Yes/no	Doc. ref.	Comments
4. Is the amount of debt forgiven in a settlement arrangement classified as loss and charged off immediately? If this is not done, does the bank treat such amounts forgiven in settlement arrangements as specific allowances? **Note:** The creation of a specific allowance is reported as a charge-off in Schedule RI-B of the call report. 5. Upon receipt of the final settlement payment, are any deficiency balances charged off within 30 days?			
Income recognition and loss allowance practices **Accrued interest and fees** 1. When determining appropriate loss allowances, does the bank evaluate the collectability of accrued interest and fees on credit card accounts? 2. If the bank does not place credit card accounts on nonaccrual, does it alternatively provide loss allowances for uncollectable fees and finance charges? 3. For banks that securitize credit card receivables, does management ensure that the owned portion of accrued interest and fees, including related estimated losses, is accounted for separately from the retained interest in accrued interest and fees from securitized accounts? **Loan-loss allowances** 4. Does bank management consider the loss inherent in both delinquent and non-delinquent loans? **Allowances for over-limit accounts** 5. Does the bank's allowance method address the additional risk associated with chronic over-limit accounts? **Note:** To be able to identify these incremental losses, it is necessary for the bank to be able to track the payment requirements and performance on over-limit accounts.			

Account Management and Loss Allowance Checklist			
	Yes/no	Doc. ref.	Comments
Allowances for workout programs			
6. Are accounts in workout programs segregated for performance measurement, impairment analysis, and monitoring purposes? (Multiple workout programs having different performance characteristics should be tracked separately.)			
7. Is the allowance allocation on workout programs at least equal to the estimated loss in each program based on historical experience as adjusted for current conditions and trends? **Note:** Adjustments should take into account changes in economic conditions, volume and mix, terms and conditions of each program, and collections.			
Recovery practices			
1. Does the bank ensure that the total amount credited to the ALLL as recoveries on a loan is limited to the amount previously charged off against the ALLL on that loan?			
Policy exceptions			
1. Does the bank allow any exceptions to the FFIEC Uniform Retail Credit Classification and Account Management Policy? If so, what types of exceptions are allowed?			
2. For exceptions granted, do the bank's policies and procedures identify the types of exceptions allowed and the circumstances for permitting them?			
3. Is the performance of accounts granted exceptions to this policy tracked and monitored?			

Appendix F: Credit Risk Model Oversight and Review Checklist

Applicability: This checklist can be used to evaluate credit risk model oversight practices for banks that use models in their retail lending business. Most of the line items pertain to credit models, but the concepts apply to all model types and can be used to evaluate general risk management practices. Examiners should consult applicable regulations as appropriate, particularly those relating to credit applications and considering a borrower's ability to pay.[102]

Note: Negative responses may indicate a higher level of risk that warrant stronger risk management practices. In such cases, further review may be necessary to determine appropriate practices to mitigate the risks.

Credit Risk Model Oversight and Review Checklist			
	Yes/no	Doc. ref.	Comments
Board and senior management oversight			
1. Have the board and senior management established an effective model risk management framework that applies to all models used in the retail lending business?			
2. Does the framework apply to the full range of models used in retail loan originations, account management, collections, portfolio management, and control systems?			
3. Does the framework include standards for model development, implementation, use, and validation?			
4. Are formal policies and procedures governing model use and oversight commensurate with retail lending's complexity, business activities, corporate culture, and overall organizational structure?			
5. Is there a clear escalation process that permits significant issues with model use and policy compliance to flow up to appropriate levels of senior management and the board?			

---

[102] For example, in connection with models used for credit applications, consider 12 CFR 1002.6, "Rules Concerning Evaluation of Applications," and 12 CFR 1026.51, "Ability to Pay" (including information in Supplement I to Part 1026 – Official Interpretations; Subpart G – Special Rules Applicable to Credit Card Accounts and Open-End Credit Offered to College Students; Section 1026.51(a)(1)(i), Consideration of Ability to Pay; Comment 5, "Information Regarding Income and Assets").

Credit Risk Model Oversight and Review Checklist			
	Yes/no	Doc. ref.	Comments
Policies and procedures			
1. Do policies require maintenance of detailed documentation of all aspects of the model risk management framework, including an inventory of models in use, results of the modeling and validation processes, and model issues and resolution?			
2. Do written policies address all aspects of model risk management, including			
a. roles and responsibilities, including staff expertise, authority, reporting lines, and continuity?			
b. governance and controls over the model risk management process?			
c. acceptable practices for model development, implementation, and use?			
d. appropriate model validation activities?			
3. Do written operating procedures specify			
a. processes used to select and retain third-party-created models, including the people who should be involved in the decisions?			
b. the prioritization, scope, and frequency of model validation?			
c. standards for the extent of validation performed before models are put into production?			
d. validation requirements for third-party models and third-party products?			
e. controls for the use of external resources for validation and compliance?			
Roles and responsibilities			
1. Does each model have a defined owner accountable for use and performance within the framework set by bank policies and procedures?			
2. Are model owners responsible for ensuring that			
• models are properly developed, implemented, and used?			
• models have undergone appropriate validation and approval processes?			
• all necessary information for validation activities is available?			
3. Do operational control processes ensure that			
• each retail model is subject to appropriate risk measurement, use limits, and monitoring?			
• appropriate resources are assigned for model validation and for guiding the scope and application of the work?			
• problems identified through validation and control systems are communicated to relevant			

Credit Risk Model Oversight and Review Checklist	Yes/no	Doc. ref.	Comments
parties throughout the organization, with a plan for corrective action? • control staff has the authority to restrict model use and monitor any limits as necessary? • when validation-work exceptions occur, other control mechanisms, such as timeliness for completing validation work and limits on model use, are established?			
Internal audit 1. Does internal audit assess the overall effectiveness of the model risk management framework for individual models and in the aggregate? 2. Are retail-model related findings documented and reported to the board or its appropriately delegated agent? 3. Does internal audit have the appropriate skills and adequate stature in the organization to assist with model risk management? 4. Does internal audit staff possess sufficient expertise to evaluate model development and use within the particular retail business lines? 5. If some internal audit staff perform validation activities, are they excluded from the assessment of the overall model risk management framework? 6. Does the internal audit scope include steps to verify that a. acceptable policies are in place, and that model owners and control groups comply with policies? b. the model inventory is accurate and complete? c. validations are performed in a timely manner and models are subject to controls that appropriately account for any weaknesses in validation activities? d. model owners and control groups are meeting documentation standards, including risk reporting?			

Credit Risk Model Oversight and Review Checklist	Yes/no	Doc. ref.	Comments

7. As part of its process reviews, does internal audit evaluate
  a. processes for establishing and monitoring limits on model use?
  b. the reliability of data used by the models?
  c. the objectivity, competence, and organizational standing of key validation participants, to determine whether those participants have the right incentives to discover and report deficiencies?
 	
8. Does internal audit review validation activities conducted by internal and external parties with the same rigor to see if those activities are conducted in accordance with prescribed standards?			

External resources
1. Are all activities performed by external service providers based on a clearly written and agreed-upon scope of work?
 	
2. Is a designated party from the bank able to understand and evaluate the results of validation and risk-control activities conducted by external parties?
 	
3. Is an internal party responsible for
  • verifying that the agreed-upon scope of work has been completed?
  • evaluating and tracking identified issues and ensuring that they are addressed?
  • making sure that completed work is incorporated into the bank's overall model risk management framework?
 	
4. Does the bank have a contingency plan in place in case the external resource is no longer available or is unsatisfactory?			

Model validation 1. Is the model validation rigor and sophistication commensurate with model use in the business and the complexity and materiality of the models?			

Credit Risk Model Oversight and Review Checklist	Yes/no	Doc. ref.	Comments
2. Is each model used in the retail lending business reviewed at least annually to determine whether it is working as intended and that the existing validation activities are sufficient?			
3. Do appropriate validation requirements apply to models developed in house as well as to those purchased from, or developed by, third parties?			
4. Do model validation exercises include the following three core elements: • Evaluation of conceptual soundness, including developmental evidence? • Ongoing monitoring, including process verification and benchmarking? • Outcomes analysis, including back-testing?			
5. Does staff doing validation work • have the requisite knowledge, skills, and expertise, including a significant degree of familiarity with the business line using the model and the model's intended use? • have no responsibility for development or use of the model and no stake in whether a model is determined to be valid? • have explicit authority to challenge model developers and to evaluate their findings, including issues and deficiencies?			
6. When model developers or users do validation work, is that work subject to critical review by an independent party who conducts additional activities to ensure proper validation?			
Model inventory 1. Does the bank maintain a comprehensive set of information for models implemented for use, under development for implementation, or recently retired?			
2. Is a specific party responsible for maintaining a company-wide inventory of all models?			
3. Is any variation of a model that warrants a separate validation included as a separate model and cross-referenced with other variations?			
4. Does the model inventory include a description of the purpose and products for which each model is designed, actual and expected usage, and any restrictions on its use?			

Credit Risk Model Oversight and Review Checklist			
	Yes/no	Doc. ref.	Comments
5. Does the model inventory indicate whether models are functioning properly, provide a description of when they were last updated, and list any exceptions to policy?			
6. Does the model inventory include the names of individuals responsible for model development and validation, the dates of completed and planned validation activities, and the period during which the model is expected to remain valid?			
Model documentation 1. Does the bank require model developers to produce effective and complete model documentation?			
2. Is model development documentation sufficiently detailed that parties unfamiliar with a model can understand how the model operates, its limitations, and its key assumptions?			
3. Does management hold model developers responsible for thorough documentation during model development, as well as for providing updates as the model and application environment changes?			
4. Do the lines of business or other decision makers document information leading to selection of a given model and its subsequent validation?			
5. When the bank uses models from a third party, is appropriate documentation of the third-party approach available so the model can be properly validated?			
6. Do validation reports articulate aspects that were reviewed, highlighting potential deficiencies over a range of financial and economic conditions, and determining whether adjustments or other compensating controls are warranted?			
7. Do validation reports include clear executive summaries, with a statement of model purpose and an accessible synopsis of model and validation results, including major limitations and key assumptions?			

Appendix G: Glossary

Ability to repay: A borrower's capacity to meet loan obligations from earnings or income. Factors generally include information such as the borrower's income, debt obligations, credit history, and monthly payments on the loan.

Adaptive control system: Credit portfolio management systems designed to reduce credit losses and increase promotional opportunities. Adaptive control systems include software that allows management to develop and analyze various strategies that take into account customer behavior and the economic environment. Also see **champion and challenger strategy**.

Add-on: An additional service or credit product sold in connection with a credit account. Examples include travel clubs, disability insurance, credit life insurance, debt suspension insurance, debt cancellation insurance, extended warranties, and fraud alert programs.

Advance rate: In financing customer purchases, the amount that a bank advances in the form of a loan in relation to the value of the underlying collateral. For example, for a new automobile, the advance rate may be calculated based on the vehicle invoice or manufacturer's suggested retail price.

Adverse selection: A disproportionately high response or acceptance rate to a marketing offer by high-risk customers in the targeted population. This situation generally occurs because the product or promotional design is flawed.

Allowance for loan and lease losses (ALLL): A contra asset account that is an estimate of uncollectible amounts (inherent losses) and is used to reduce the book value of loans and leases to the amount that is expected to be collected. The ALLL is established and maintained by charges against the bank's operating income, i.e., the provision expense.

Amortization: The process of paying off a loan by gradually reducing the balance through a series of installment payments.

Application scoring: The use of a statistical model to objectively score credit applications and predict likely performance.

Attrition: The loss of accounts either involuntarily, because of bad debts, death, etc., or voluntarily, at the option of the accountholder.

Broker: An individual or company that sources customers for loans and then places those loans with banks for funding.

Buy rate: The interest rate a bank charges for loans purchased through third-party dealers. Used in indirect lending.

Captive finance company: The financing arm of a manufacturing firm or other company that is used to finance the sale of the company's products. For example, the financing arm of an automobile manufacturer, such as Ford Motor Credit Co.

Champion and challenger strategy: A structured process for testing and comparing business rules and decision criteria before full-scale production changes. The "champion" strategy is the strategy or decision process currently used in production (that is, applied to most accounts in the normal course of business), while one or more "challenger" strategies are simultaneously applied to smaller test groups to evaluate results in a controlled manner. The results of the challenger strategies are compared against those of the champion to determine whether to install a new champion.

Chronology log: A chronological record of internal and external events relevant to the credit function.

Closed-end: A loan or extension of credit made for a predetermined amount, at a fixed or variable interest rate, with periodic payments of principal and interest over a specified term. Generally, the required payments pay off the loan in full by the end of the term. In some cases, the amortization schedule extends past the maturity date, leaving a lump sum (or balloon) payment due upon maturity.

Coincident: Refers to end-of-period delinquencies and losses in relation to total as of the same date. Distinguished from vintage, lagged, and other time series measures.

Consumer credit counseling (CCC): Service offered by nonprofit agencies that counsel overextended consumers and is funded by bank "fair share" contributions (a negotiated percentage of the consumer's payment to the bank). CCC entities work with consumers and their banks to develop a budget and a debt repayment plan. Banks generally offer concessions to customers in CCC programs.

Consumer reporting agency: Any entity that, for monetary fees, dues, or on a cooperative nonprofit basis, regularly engages in whole or in part in the practice of assembling or evaluating consumer credit information or other information on consumers for the purpose of furnishing consumer reports to third parties, and that uses any means or facility of interstate commerce for the purpose of preparing or furnishing consumer reports.

Control function: Those functions that have a responsibility to provide independent and objective assessment, reporting, and assurance. Examples include risk review, compliance, internal audit, and loan review.

Corporate governance: A set of relationships among a company's management, its board, its shareholders, and other stakeholders. Corporate governance also provides the structure through which the objectives of the company are set, and by which the means of attaining those objectives and monitoring performance are determined.

Credit bureau: A consumer reporting agency that is a clearinghouse for information on the credit ratings of individuals or businesses. The three largest credit bureaus in the United States are Equifax, Experian, and TransUnion.

Credit report: Report from a consumer reporting agency providing a consumer's credit history. Credit reports are convenient and inexpensive for banks to obtain because large users typically pay lower rates than small users. Mortgage lenders usually require more thorough and detailed credit reports than lenders making small retail loans. A merged credit report contains files from the three major credit bureaus.

Credit scoring: A statistical method for predicting the creditworthiness of applicants and existing customers.

Cross-selling: The use of one product or service as a base for selling additional products and services.

Cure programs: A process where a delinquent loan is returned to current status without the borrower paying all past-due amounts. Borrowers must typically demonstrate the willingness and ability to meet current obligations, but an inability to catch up with past missed payments.

Dealer: The retail outlet for automobile or manufactured housing sales. Dealers take loan applications from their customers and "shop" them to banks for approval and funding.

Dealer reserve: Bank-controlled, dealer-specific deposit accounts used to accumulate the difference, when applicable, between the interest rate paid by borrowers on indirect installment loans and the rate at which the bank purchased the contracts from the dealers (see **buy rate**). Collected funds are released to the dealers according to the terms of the dealer agreements.

Debt cancellation insurance: A loan term or contractual arrangement modifying loan terms under which a bank agrees to cancel all or part of a customer's obligation to repay an extension of credit from that bank upon the occurrence of a specified event.

Debt service: A measure of a customer's income in relation to committed debt payments.

Debt suspension agreement: A loan term or contractual arrangement modifying loan terms under which a bank agrees to suspend all or part of a customer's obligation to repay an extension of credit from that bank upon the occurrence of a specified event. The term "debt suspension agreement" does not include loan payment deferral arrangements in which the triggering event is the borrower's unilateral election to defer repayment, or the bank's unilateral decision to allow a deferral of repayment.

Debt-to-income ratio: The ratio calculated by using identified monthly debt obligations or payments (for example, home mortgage, automobile, and credit card) as the numerator and identified monthly income amounts or receipts as the denominator.

Deferral: Deferring a contractually due payment on a closed-end loan without affecting the other terms, including maturity, of the loan.

Due diligence: An investigation or audit of a potential investment, generally designed to confirm all material facts in regards to a sale. Also refers to the general care a reasonable person should take before entering into an agreement or a transaction with another party.

Effective challenge: Critical analysis by objective, informed parties who can identify limitations and assumptions and produce appropriate changes.

Extension: Extending monthly payments on a closed-end loan and rolling back the maturity by the number of months extended. The account is shown as current upon granting the extension. If extension fees are assessed, they should be collected at the time of the extension and not added to the balance of the loan.

Fixed payment programs (cure programs): Also described as workout programs, these include CCC and in-bank programs designed to help customers work through some type of temporary or permanent financial impairment. Cure programs typically involve a reduced payment for a specified period of time and may also include interest rate concessions.

Forbearance: A lender's decision not to exercise a legally enforceable right against a borrower in default, in exchange for a promise to make regular payments in the future.

High-side override: A denied loan that meets or exceeds the established credit score cutoff. To compute a bank's high-side override rate, divide the number of declines scoring at or above the cutoff score by the total number of applicants scoring at or above the cutoff.

Indirect lending: A process in which a bank purchases loan contracts from a dealer or retailer as a holder in due course and collects principal and interest payments from the borrower. Banks typically purchase installment contracts at a discount from face value on the notes.

Inherent losses: The amount of loss that meets the conditions of ASC 450 for accrual of a loss contingency (i.e., a provision to the ALLL).

Interest-only loan: A loan on which the borrower is required to pay only interest, and not any of the loan principal, for a specified period of time. The specified time can be for the full loan term, or for a limited time after which amortizing payments are required.

Internal controls: A process for assuring achievement of an organization's objectives in operational effectiveness and efficiency, reliable financial reporting, and compliance with laws, regulations, and policies.

Lagged analysis: Analysis that minimizes the effects of growth. Lagged analysis uses the current balance of the item of interest as the numerator (e.g., loans past due 30 days or more), and the outstanding balance of the portfolio being measured for some earlier time period as the denominator (generally six or 12 months before).

Low-side override: An approved loan that fails to meet the credit scoring criteria. To compute the low-side override rate, divide the number of approvals scoring below the cutoff credit score by the total number of applicants scoring below the cutoff.

Loss mitigation: Loan collection techniques used to reduce or eliminate the possible loss.

Managed assets: Total balance sheet assets plus all off-book securitized assets.

Negative amortization: An increase in the loan balance that occurs when a loan payment is insufficient to cover the interest and fees due and payable for the payment period and the resulting deficient amount is capitalized into the loan's balance.

Open-end: Consumer credit extended by a creditor under a plan in which the creditor reasonably contemplates repeated transactions; the creditor may impose a finance charge from time to time, according to the agreement with the borrowers, on an outstanding unpaid balance; and the amount of credit that may be extended to the consumer during the term of the plan (up to any limit set by the creditor) is generally made available to the extent that any payment due is made, as contractually agreed.

Pay-ahead: Keeping track of excess payment amounts and reducing the next consecutive payment(s) accordingly. As a result, the customer is not required by the bank to make payments until the amount of the overage has been extinguished. For example, if a customer's automobile payment is $200 per month and the customer remits $600, the next payment is not due until the third subsequent month. Pay-aheads can pose increased risk, because they do not require a minimum payment every month. When banks require customers to make monthly payments, it enables the banks to monitor portfolio quality through more accurate delinquency reporting. Banks should limit the use of pay-aheads to accounts with low risk characteristics. Banks that accept pay-aheads on credit card accounts must refer to 12 CFR 1026.53, which sets forth the requirements for the allocation of the excess payment amounts.

Payment holidays (skip-a-pay): The practice of giving the bank's most creditworthy customers the option of forgoing or skipping payments for a given month. Interest continues to accrue for the skipped time period. Payment holidays are sometimes offered as frequently as twice a year, and usually coincide with summer vacations, late-summer back-to-school shopping, or December holidays. This practice may be imprudent when offered broadly for some products or customers, and should be used judiciously.

Penalty pricing: Increased loan or line finance charge imposed when a borrower fails to pay as agreed, based on performance criteria in the loan or cardholder agreement. Penalty pricing is subject to the Credit Card Accountability Responsibility and Disclosure Act and Regulation Z requirements and limitations.

Point of sale: The place where sales are made. For retail credit this is typically the area where a customer completes a transaction, such as a checkout counter.

Prepayment: The payment of all or part of a loan before it is contractually due.

Prescreen (preapprove): To score or otherwise qualify a list of names or defined credit bureau population using credit bureau information with the intent of making a firm offer of credit to those meeting the criteria. Under the Fair Credit Reporting Act, the issuer generally is required to make a firm offer of credit to the consumers it solicits for a credit card; otherwise, under the act, the issuer would not have a permissible purpose for obtaining the prescreened list (with limited exceptions).

Price points: The price tiers into which banks segment retail portfolios. Price points show rates and outstandings in each tier. Especially important when teaser rates are offered, price points enable banks to model past, present, and future revenue and the impact of shifts that result from pricing strategies. Some banks identify three tiers, such as low-rate teasers, medium-rate standard products, and high-yield loans.

Promise to pay: A term used in collection departments to describe customers who have been contacted regarding their delinquent accounts and have committed to remitting a payment. Once the payment is received, it would be reported under "promises kept."

Quality assurance: The process of evaluating the planned and systematic actions necessary to provide adequate confidence that loan originations and credit administration practices will satisfy given quality requirements.

Quality control: The process of assuring that loans (or processes) conform to established standards of quality.

Re-age: Returning a delinquent, open-end account to current status without collecting the total amount of principal, interest, and fees that are contractually due.

Renewal: Underwriting a matured, closed-end loan, generally at its outstanding principal amount and on similar terms.

Repossession: Seizure of collateral securing a loan in default.

Retail credit: Open- and closed-end credit extended to individuals for household, family, and other personal expenditures. Retail credit includes consumer loans, credit cards, and loans to individuals secured by their personal residences, including first mortgage, home equity, and home improvement loans.

Rewrite: Underwriting an existing loan by significantly changing its terms, including payment amounts, interest rates, amortization schedules, or final maturity.

Right-party contacts: Communicating directly with the borrower, or someone who is legally designated to make decisions for the borrower, such as a person with a power of attorney.

Risk appetite: Refers to the aggregate level and types of risk the board and senior management are willing to assume to achieve the bank's strategic objectives and business plan, consistent with applicable capital, liquidity, and other regulatory requirements.

Risk attractiveness: An extension of risk preferences. Risk attractiveness describes how current economic and business conditions affect the relative attractiveness of risks, and how that translates into current strategies and business plans.

Risk governance framework: A part of the corporate governance framework, through which the board and management establish and make decisions about the bank's strategy and risk approach; articulate and monitor adherence to risk appetite and risk limits through the bank's strategy; and identify, measure, monitor, and control risks.

Risk layering: The practice of assuming high levels of risk in more than one loan underwriting or loan structure characteristic. For example, originating a mortgage loan in which the borrower's credit score is at or near the minimum acceptable level and the LTV ratio is at or near the maximum level permissible. Both may be within policy limits, but the combination results in higher risk than if only one factor was near its policy limit.

Risk limit: A method of authorizing specific forms of risk taking. Risk limits generally consist of three factors: (1) a risk metric, (2) a risk measure, and (3) a limit that should not be breached. For retail credit, risk limits are often set at the product, business line, or significant segment (e.g., by credit score, geography, and industry) levels. Risk limits can be notional amounts, or set in relation to other measures such as regulatory capital or economic capital.

Risk management: A structured approach to identifying, monitoring, measuring, and managing exposures to reduce the potential impact of an uncertain event happening.

Risk preferences: The key risks a bank chooses to pursue to achieve its mission.

Risk profile: A point-in-time assessment of a bank's risks, aggregated within and across each relevant risk category.

Risk strategies: Strategic expression of the bank's overall philosophy to pursuing and assuming the risks necessary to achieve the bank's mission and align risk taking within the business lines.

Risk tolerances: A quantitative expression of the key metrics that define the aggregate amount of risk the bank will tolerate over varying time horizons. Risk tolerances should be measurable and possible to monitor.

Roll rate: Measure of the movement of accounts and balances from one payment status to another (e.g., percentage of accounts or dollars that were current last month rolling to 30 days past due this month).

Scenario analysis: Assessing the potential outcome of various scenarios by setting up possible situations and analyzing the potential outcomes of each situation. Also known as "what if" analysis.

Securitization: The process of creating an investment security backed by credit card receivables, mortgages, installment loans, or other loans.

Stress testing: Analysis that estimates the effect of economic changes or other changes on key bank performance measures (e.g., losses, delinquencies, and profitability). Key variables used in stress testing could include interest rates, score distributions, asset values, growth rates, and unemployment rates.

Subprime lending: Extending credit to borrowers who exhibit characteristics indicating a significantly higher risk of default than traditional bank lending customers.

Teaser or introductory rate: Temporary interest rate offered by lenders to consumers as an incentive to open accounts with the lenders. The teaser period generally lasts anywhere between six months to one year. Customers' accounts revert to standard rate pricing after the introductory period. Credit card issuers must comply with the requirements of 12 CFR 1026.55(b)(1), "Limitations on Increasing Annual Percentage Rates, Fees, and Charges," when offering a temporary rate.

Vintage analysis: Grouping loans by origination time period (e.g., quarter) for analysis purposes. Performance trends are tracked for each vintage and compared with other vintages with similar time on book.

Appendix H: Abbreviations

ALLL	allowance for loan and lease losses
AML	anti-money laundering
ASC	Accounting Standards Codification
ATR	ability to repay
BSA	Bank Secrecy Act
CCC	consumer credit counseling
CEO	chief executive officer
CFR	Code of Federal Regulations
FFIEC	Federal Financial Institutions Examination Council
GAAP	generally accepted accounting principles
HELOC	home equity line of credit
ICQ	internal control questionnaire
LTV	loan-to-value
MIS	management information systems
OCC	Office of the Comptroller of the Currency
OTS	Office of Thrift Supervision
RCCP	retail credit classification and account management policy
TDR	troubled debt restructuring
USC	U.S. Code

References

Federal Consumer Protection Laws and Implementing Regulations

10 USC 987 and 32 CFR 232, "Military Lending Act"

12 USC 2601 and 12 CFR 1024 (Regulation X), "Real Estate Settlement Procedures Act"

15 USC 1601 et seq. and 12 CFR 1026 (Regulation Z), "Truth in Lending Act"

15 USC 1639 et seq. and 12 CFR 1026, "Home Ownership and Equity Protection Act"

15 USC 1681 et seq., "Fair Credit Reporting Act," as amended by the Fair and Accurate Credit Transactions Act of 2003; 12 CFR 1022, "Fair Credit Reporting (Regulation V)"

15 USC 1691 et seq. and 12 CFR 1002 (Regulation B), "Equal Credit Opportunity Act"

15 USC 1692 et seq. and 12 CFR 1006 (Regulation F), "Fair Debt Collection Practices Act"

15 USC 6801 et seq. and 12 CFR 1016 (Regulation P), "Privacy of Consumer Financial Information Act"

15 USC 7001 et seq., "Electronic Signatures in Global and National Commerce Act"

42 USC 3601 et seq., "Fair Housing Act"; 24 CFR 100.1 et seq., "Discriminatory Conduct Under the Fair Housing Act"

50 USC, appendix 501, et seq., "Servicemembers Civil Relief Act"

Other Laws and Regulations Applicable to Retail Lending

Laws

12 USC 24, "Corporate Powers of Associations"

12 USC 85, "Rate of Interest on Loans, Discounts and Purchases"

12 USC 1464(c), "Loans and Investments

12 USC 5531, "Prohibiting Unfair, Deceptive, or Abusive Acts or Practices"

12 USC 5536, "Prohibited Acts"

15 USC 45, "Federal Trade Commission Act"

31 USC 5311 et seq., "Bank Secrecy Act"

Regulations

National Banks and Federal Savings Associations

12 CFR 3 subpart C (12 CFR 3.20–3.22), "Definition of Capital"

12 CFR 3 subpart D (12 CFR 3.30–3.63) "Risk-Weighted Assets-Standardized Approach" and subpart E (12 CFR 3.100–3.173), "Risk-Weighted Assets – Internal Ratings-Based and Advanced Measurement Approaches"

12 CFR 21.21, "Procedures for Monitoring Bank Secrecy Act (BSA) Compliance"

12 CFR 30, "Safety and Soundness Standards"

12 CFR 34, subpart C, "Appraisals"

12 CFR 41, subpart I, "Proper Disposal of Records Containing Consumer Information" and subpart J, "Identity Theft Red Flags"

National Banks

12 CFR 7.4001, "Charging Interest by National Banks at Rates Permitted Competing Institutions; Charging Interest to Corporate Borrowers"

12 CFR 7.4002, "National Bank Charges"

12 CFR 7.4008, "Lending by National Banks"

12 CFR 21.11, "Suspicious Activity Reports"

12 CFR 23, "Leasing"

12 CFR 37, "Debt Cancellation Contracts and Debt Suspension Agreements"

Federal Savings Associations

12 CFR 7.4010, "Applicability of State Law and Visitorial Powers to Federal Savings Associations and Subsidiaries"

12 CFR 128, "Nondiscrimination Requirements"

12 CFR 160, "Lending and Investment"

12 CFR 162, "Regulatory Reporting Standards"

12 CFR 163.176, "Interest-Rate-Risk-Management Procedures"

12 CFR 163.180, "Suspicious Activity Reports and Other Reports and Statements"

Comptroller's Handbook

Consumer Compliance

"Compliance Management System"

"Fair Credit Reporting"

"Fair Lending"

"Other Consumer Protection Laws and Regulations"

"Privacy of Consumer Financial Information"

"Real Estate Settlement Procedures Act"

"SAFE Act"

"Servicemembers Civil Relief Act of 2003"

"Truth in Lending Act"

Examination Process

"Bank Supervision Process"

"Community Bank Supervision"

"Federal Branches and Agencies Supervision"

"Large Bank Supervision"

"Sampling Methodologies"

Safety and Soundness, Asset Quality

"Allowance for Loan and Lease Losses"

"Concentrations of Credit"

"Credit Card Lending"

"Deposit-Related Credit"

"Installment Lending"

"Loan Portfolio Management"

"Mortgage Banking"

"Rating Credit Risk"
"Residential Real Estate Lending"
"Student Lending"

Safety and Soundness, Liquidity
"Liquidity"
"Asset Securitization"

Safety and Soundness, Management
"Corporate and Risk Governance"
"Internal and External Audits"
"Internal Control"

Safety and Soundness, Other Activities
"Merchant Processing"

Safety and Soundness, Sensitivity to Market Risk
"Interest Rate Risk"

Office of Thrift Supervision Examination Handbook

Section 209, "Sampling" (November 2010)
Section 221, "Asset-Backed Securitization" (September 2003)
Section 340, "Internal Control" (October 2009)
Section 760, "New Activities and Services" (September 2009)
Section 1300, "Fair Credit Reporting Act" (January 2011)

OCC Issuances

Advisory Letters
Advisory Letter 2000-7, "Abusive Lending Practices" (July 25, 2000)
Advisory Letter 2000-11, "Title Loan Programs" (November 27, 2000)
    (not yet applicable to federal savings associations)
Advisory Letter 2002-3, "Guidance on Unfair or Deceptive Acts or Practices"
    (March 22, 2002)
Advisory Letter 2003-2, "Guidelines for National Banks to Guard Against Predatory and
    Abusive Lending Practices" (February 21, 2003)
Advisory Letter 2003-3, "Avoiding Predatory and Abusive Lending Practices in
    Brokered and Purchased Loans" (February 21, 2003)

OCC Bulletins
OCC Bulletin 1997-24, "Credit Scoring Models: Examination Guidance" (May 20, 1997)
OCC Bulletin 1999-10, "Subprime Lending Activities" (March 5, 1999)
OCC Bulletin 1999-15, "Subprime Lending: Risks and Rewards" (April 5, 1999)
    (not applicable to federal savings associations)

OCC Bulletin 1999-38, "Interagency Guidelines for Real Estate Lending Policies: Treatment of High LTV Residential Real Estate Loans" (October 13, 1999)

OCC Bulletin 1999-46, "Interagency Guidance on Asset Securitization Activities: Asset Securitization" (December 13, 1999)

OCC Bulletin 2000-3, "Consumer Credit Reporting Practices: FFIEC Advisory Letter" (February 16, 2000)

OCC Bulletin 2000-20, "Uniform Retail Credit Classification and Account Management Policy: Policy Implementation" (June 20, 2000)

OCC Bulletin 2001-6, "Subprime Lending: Expanded Guidance for Subprime Lending Programs" (January 31, 2001)

OCC Bulletin 2001-37, "Policy Statement on Allowance for Loan and Lease Losses Methodologies and Documentation for Banks and Savings Institutions: ALLL Methodologies and Documentation" (July 20, 2001)

OCC Bulletin 2002-16, "Bank Use of Foreign-Based Third-Party Service Providers: Risk Management Guidance" (May 15, 2002)

OCC Bulletin 2002-40, "Debt Cancellation Contracts and Debt Suspension Agreements: Final Rule," (October 16, 2002) (not applicable to federal savings associations)

OCC Bulletin 2003-1, "Credit Card Lending: Account Management and Loss Allowance Guidance" (January 8, 2003)

OCC Bulletin 2004-20, "Risk Management of New, Expanded, or Modified Bank Products and Services: Risk Management Process" (May 10, 2004) (national banks; for federal savings associations, refer to the *OTS Examination Handbook*, section 760, "New Activities and Services" (September 2009))

OCC Bulletin 2005-22, "Home Equity Lending: Credit Risk Management Guidance" (May 16, 2005)

OCC Bulletin 2006-34, "Gift Card Disclosures: Guidance on Disclosure and Marketing Issues" (August 14, 2006)

OCC Bulletin 2006-43, "Home Equity Lending: Addendum to OCC Bulletin 2005-22" (October 4, 2006)

OCC Bulletin 2006-47, "Allowance for Loan and Lease Losses (ALLL): Guidance and Frequently Asked Questions (FAQs) on the ALLL" (December 13, 2006)

OCC Bulletin 2007-45, "Identity Theft Red Flags and Address Discrepancies: Final Rulemaking" (November 14, 2007)

OCC Bulletin 2008-28, "Fair Credit Reporting Act (FCRA): Additions to FCRA Examination Procedures" (October 15, 2008)

OCC Bulletin 2009-23, "Fair Credit Reporting: Accuracy and Integrity of Consumer Report Information and Direct Consumer Dispute Regulations and Guidelines: Final Rule and Guidelines Together with Advanced Notice of Proposed Rulemaking" (July 20, 2009) (not applicable to federal savings associations)

OCC Bulletin 2010-24, "Incentive Compensation: Interagency Guidance on Sound Incentive Compensation Policies" (June 30, 2010)

OCC Bulletin 2010-25, "Property Assessed Clean Energy (PACE) Programs: Supervisory Guidance" (July 6, 2010)

OCC Bulletin 2010-42, "Sound Practices for Appraisals and Evaluations: Interagency Appraisal and Evaluation Guidelines" (December 10, 2010)

OCC Bulletin 2011-12, "Sound Practices for Model Risk Management: Supervisory Guidance on Model Risk Management" (April 4, 2011)

OCC Bulletin 2011-16, "Servicemembers Civil Relief Act: Revised Examination Procedures" (May 3, 2011)

OCC Bulletin 2012-6, "Interagency Guidance on ALLL Estimation Practices for Junior Liens: Guidance on Junior Liens" (January 31, 2012)

OCC Bulletin 2012-10, "Troubled Debt Restructurings: Supervisory Guidance on Accounting and Reporting Requirements" (April 5, 2012)

OCC Bulletin 2012-14, "Stress Testing: Interagency Stress Testing Guidance" (May 14, 2012)

OCC Bulletin 2012-33, "Community Bank Stress Testing: Supervisory Guidance," (October 18, 2012)

OCC Bulletin 2012-41, "Stress Testing: Final Rule for Dodd–Frank Act Section 165(i)" (December 20, 2012)

OCC Bulletin 2013-29, "Third-Party Relationships: Risk Management Guidance" (October 30, 2013)

OCC Bulletin 2013-40, "Deposit Advance Products: Final Supervisory Guidance" (December 26, 2013)

OCC Bulletin 2014-4, "Secured Consumer Debt Discharged in Chapter 7 Bankruptcy: Supervisory Expectations" (February 14, 2014)

OCC Bulletin 2014-5, "Dodd–Frank Stress Testing: Supervisory Guidance for Banking Organizations With Total Consolidated Assets of More Than $10 Billion but Less Than $50 Billion" (March 5, 2014)

OCC Bulletin 2014-29, "Risk Management of Home Equity Lines of Credit Approaching the End-of-Draw Periods: Interagency Guidance" (July 1, 2014)

OCC Bulletin 2014-37, "Consumer Debt Sales: Risk Management Guidance" (August 4, 2014)

OCC Bulletin 2014-42, "Credit Practices Rules: Interagency Guidance Regarding Unfair or Deceptive Credit Practices" (August 22, 2014)

OCC Bulletin 2014-45, "Heightened Standards for Large Banks; Integration of 12 CFR 30 and 12 CFR 170: Final Rules and Guidelines" (September 25, 2014)

OCC Bulletin 2015-7, "Student Loans: Interagency Guidance on Private Student Loans With Graduated Repayment Terms at Origination" (January 29, 2015)

OCC Bulletin 2015-17, "Deposit-Related Credit: Revised Comptroller's Handbook Booklet" (March 6, 2015)

OCC Bulletin 2015-36, "Tax Refund-Related Products: Risk Management Guidance" (August 4, 2015)

Other

Financial Accounting Standards Board's Accounting Standards Codification
ASC 310, "Receivables"
ASC 326, "Financial Instruments – Credit Losses"
ASC 450, "Contingencies"
ASC 810, "Consolidations"
ASC 840, "Leases"

ASC 860, "Transfers and Servicing"

ASC Subtopic 450-20, "Loss Contingencies"

Emerging Issues Task Force 00-21, "Revenue Arrangements with Multiple Deliverables"

Emerging Issues Task Force 00-22, "Accounting for 'Points' and Certain Other Time-Based or Volume-Based Sales Incentive Offers and Offers for Free Products or Services to Be Delivered in the Future"

Emerging Issues Task Force 01-09, "Accounting for Consideration Given by a Vendor to a Customer (Including a Reseller of the Vendor's Products)"

FFIEC

FFIEC Bank Secrecy Act/Anti-Money Laundering Examination Manual

FFIEC Information Technology Examination Handbook

OCC

An Examiner's Guide to Problem Bank Identification, Rehabilitation, and Resolution (January 2001)

Bank Accounting Advisory Series

www.ingramcontent.com/pod-product-compliance
Lightning Source LLC
Chambersburg PA
CBHW081150180526
45170CB00006B/2004